C/W

CAREERS
WORKING OUTDOORS
Judith Humphries

Fourth Edition

KOGAN PAGE
CAREERS
SERIES

First published in 1982
Second edition 1985
Third edition 1987
Fourth edition 1991

Kogan Page Limited
120 Pentonville Road
London N1 9JN

British Library Cataloguing in Publication Data

A CIP record for this book is available from the British Library.

ISBN 0-7494-0524-4

Printed and bound in Great Britain by Biddles Limited, Guildford and King's Lynn

Contents

Introduction

Many people work outdoors. Bricklayers, traffic wardens and footballers all spend much of their working life in the open air. This book, however, is not about such people. It is concerned with the essential spirit of the world outdoors: the natural environment. It is a book for people who like growing things, or who are interested in nature and would like to make their contribution to maintaining its beauty and balance, both for its own sake and so that it can be enjoyed by the public.

The field is dominated by three large industries – agriculture, horticulture and forestry which, between them, employ more people than any other single industry in the British Isles. There are considerable prospects, too, in amenity horticulture, which is concerned with the upkeep of parks and public open spaces, and interesting opportunities in conservation work. A small, but rewarding area of work is rural crafts, often rooted in ancient tradition and experiencing new popularity in recent years. Jobs concerned with all these aspects of the outdoors, for people whose qualifications range from a few GCSE/CSEs to higher degrees, are described in Part 1, and courses and training schemes are listed in Part 2.

If you are interested in a job which will keep you outdoors, it is important that you ask yourself a few questions about your ability to cope with the working conditions. You will be outside all year round, and not just when the sun is shining or the weather pleasantly mild. There is a certain amount of hard physical labour, especially in forestry, and you must be competent to work with machinery as well as with your hands. Your work will be dictated by the seasons and you will have very busy times when you must be able to work under pressure and slacker ones when routine, sometimes monotonous, tasks are carried out. But the work is never dull for long: the sun *does* shine and many people can work close to nature in the most pleasant of environments.

5

All the jobs described in this book are available to both men and women, though, traditionally, the field has been male dominated and continues to be so. Everyone I spoke to thought a woman could do the work, even in forestry where physical demands are probably the greatest. Several people pointed out that endurance rather than strength is the quality most needed, and women can often endure more than men.

The availability of work will depend on where you are. If you are willing to move away from home, you will sometimes find that accommodation is provided by the employer. If this does not appeal, you should still have a fair choice of work outdoors, even if you live in a town or city.

One of the problems people with higher qualifications face is that promotion usually means leaving the outdoors and proceeding to a managerial office job. However, there are a few opportunities, notably in conservation and experimental farming or horticulture, where the work remains close to its practical base. In all cases, people involved in managerial work must have a sound practical experience of their subject.

Many people are determined to spend their whole working lives out of doors and this does not mean a lifetime spent in unskilled labour. Skill is needed for almost all of the work and this is recognised by the provision of government-sponsored craft training and apprenticeship schemes in agriculture, horticulture and forestry. Theoretically, training is available for everybody, whatever their academic achievement, and while the reality is not always quite like this, it is an appropriately egalitarian ideal for careers working outdoors. Before nature, we are all equal.

Part 1

Chapter 1
Agriculture

Introduction

Agriculture can be defined as the large-scale raising of crops and animals to provide food. This chapter is about the structure and training arrangements of agriculture generally, but more particularly about arable farming, which is concerned with the raising of crops. Much has been written about factory farming – the practice of raising animals in intensive and unnatural conditions – and I need add no more as it falls outside the scope of this book. If you are interested in stockraising, either by modern, or more traditional methods, you could consult *Careers Working with Animals* by Helen Young in the Kogan Page careers series.

Agriculture is the single largest industry in the British Isles and, despite increased mechanisation, provides employment for more than 300,000 full-time workers, though up to 100,000 jobs could be lost in agriculture before the end of the century. It is an essential industry because of its role in the provision of our food and, for this reason, farming has a government department of its own administering grants to farmers, an extensive advisory service, research projects and a few experimental farms. Apart from a few government-sponsored projects and the activities of a few large chemical companies such as Fisons and ICI, all farming is in private hands.

The Farming Life

Farming has become a way of life for many people across several generations. Farms are passed on from parents to children and whole families engage in agricultural work. But do not allow this to put you off if you do not come from a farming background. It is quite possible for outsiders, either from an urban or rural area, to enter agriculture, and for those who find a job, the prospects are interesting and varied. But you must understand what you are letting yourself in for.

For a start, you will live in the country, probably at a distance from any large centre of population, and you will be at the beck and call of the seasons. Nature does not wait for anyone, and whether you are involved with animals or crops, there will be busy times when tasks must be finished however tired you are, or however bad the weather. This is no 9 to 5 job, and you must be prepared to work at any time of night or day. You must be ready to do the dirty jobs: muck-spreading, working on the land when it is deep in mud, handling silage whose pervasive smell you may or may not like. But you must be clean and disciplined; disease can spread rapidly among plants or animals on a disorganised farm.

Training

All agricultural work demands a measure of knowledge and skill and this is reflected in the training available. It extends from the provision of apprenticeship schemes and proficiency tests for people who want to learn on the job and gain a craftsman's certificate, through a variety of full-time courses at agricultural colleges, to university degrees. As agriculture is a practical pursuit, all people taking academic courses must spend a year gaining general farm experience before they begin their studies.

The agricultural colleges are the backbone of the training system and are widespread throughout the British Isles. The training offered in each will vary in content, and as full-time courses are residential, you can move away from home to take the course of your choice. In fact, staff at agricultural colleges say they prefer students to branch out in this way as it widens their perspectives for the future.

Arable Farming

No one farm is like another. Farmers are different and the land is different too. In upland areas, the poorer soil is best suited to raising animals and in the more fertile lowland areas rainfall is the main factor governing the choice of farming. The wetter, western half of Britain favours dairy farming and in the drier eastern half cereal crops flourish. So the type of farming you do will depend largely on where you are prepared to work. You will find arable farming concentrated in the lower areas of Britain, particularly the east. Lincolnshire College of Agriculture runs specialist courses in arable farming because it is situated in the centre of this activity.

Working on arable land entails similar activities, whatever crop is grown. You will be involved in the round of cultivation – preparing the land, sowing the seed, caring for the crop and, finally, harvesting it. Then the crop must be sorted and prepared for marketing. In all these tasks, your first concern must be for the soil; choosing the right crops and rotating them so that the land maintains its richness. The main danger in arable farming is making the land impoverished by using it too intensively.

Arable work is far more mechanised than stockraising and the most important machine is the tractor. Almost all operations in arable work can be carried out mechanically, usually with the help of a tractor. If tractor driving appeals to you and you are able to manage the variety of implements used today, you will probably enjoy arable farming. But you must remember that there are no warm barns or cosy animal houses to escape to when the weather is bad. Arable farming, apart from the shelter a tractor affords, is truly an outside job – in all weathers. However, it does not tie you down as much as stockraising. Unlike animals, crops do not demand attention every day of the week in the year. Nor do they have their crises during unsocial night hours.

Being a Farmer

A farmer is one who runs a farm. Most farmers own their land but there are a few opportunities for suitably qualified and experienced people to become tenant farmers or work as farm managers. Unfortunately, these jobs are not often available, as many tenancies are secure and remain in one family, and management positions are few and far between.

Training for Management

Landowners offering a tenancy or a management post will want to make sure that their land is well farmed, and so they will usually seek a qualified person for the job. The appropriate qualifications are a BTEC National Diploma (ND) or, if you wish to combine technological and managerial training with the practical, a BTEC Higher National Diploma (HND), or a degree. Details of courses leading to these awards are given in Part 2. All courses have entrance requirements which demand some measure of academic success at school.

If you seek a management position, you will usually be required to follow your training with some practical experience. Some larger employers run their own management courses to bridge this gap. Addresses are given in Part 2.

Even if you are lucky enough to expect to farm your own land, it is sensible to ensure that you have a thorough training. Farming is a scientific, as well as a practical activity, and as it is a commercial enterprise, requires business and management skills. All these aspects are covered in the courses listed above. However, these alone are not enough. Experience counts, and it is essential, whatever your academic qualifications, to spend a few years in general agricultural work before attempting to set out on your own.

Case Study

A Farmer talks about his work

Peter owns a small mixed farm and does most of the work himself. Like many farmers nowadays, he uses agricultural contractors to help him during the busiest times.

It costs a packet these days to get into farming by buying your own farm. In my case, I was lucky. I got a job on a farm and took a course in agriculture and afterwards (there's a hell of a lot of luck in life) my father-in-law set me up.

I was on my own after three years' working on a biggish farm – 1,500 acres – and I learnt a lot from that farmer. He used to say that the best manure was the farmer's boots. He reckoned a farmer should walk the complete farm at least once a week, and even with his large acreage he used to do it. That way, you know everything that's happening: what needs attention, what's doing well, or not so well, and you memorise it and take action accordingly.

No two farms are the same. By knowing your land well, you learn about your individual fields. Even on this small farm, I've got sandy soils and clay soils and each needs completely different treatment. You must respect your land. By farming too intensively, or repeating the same crops for too long, you can rob the soil. You can put chemicals into it, but without humus, or texture, it's no good. You need a lot of knowledge to manage these things – knowledge plus experience.

There are advantages in mixed farming. For all the new technology, there's nothing that can beat the combination of animals and crops as far as the soil is concerned. My farm is 104 acres and I keep 30 head of beef stock and 80–90 ewes which produce an average of

140 lambs each year. I grow 25 acres of corn from which I harvest about 33 tons, and I sometimes grow a cash crop like swedes or turnips. They are useful because you can always feed them to the animals if you don't find a buyer. We also keep free-range poultry, but they lay too many eggs in other people's gardens to be a commercial proposition.

This is not intensive farming but I prefer it this way. I would have to specialise more and use the land far harder to make it economical to employ permanent labour. A lot of farmers are in this position and it's bad for farm labourers, I know. But not all of us want to run a high-powered commercial enterprise. Farmers are individualists and farming is a way of life.

The Farm Worker

If your interests and talents are practical, and if you do not wish to be involved with the theoretical and managerial side of farming, you are best advised to find a job as a farm worker and then take one of the practical training schemes available. All farm work demands skill and a basic knowledge of the principles behind it. A reliable and experienced farm worker can, on a large farm, progress to a supervisory position, either having charge of other workers or assuming responsibility for one aspect of the farm's activities. In each case, you will spend your time outside and will not be involved with paperwork.

Training

Information about training in agriculture is available from local Agricultural Training Board offices; the address of your nearest office will be found in the telephone directory. The local Jobcentre, careers office and TEC (Training and Enterprise Council), as well as agricultural colleges, should also be able to supply information about training opportunities. Training is often geared to local needs, and the courses available at local colleges. If you want to specialise in an area of agriculture that does not have training offered by local colleges, it may be necessary to apply to one outside your area – but there may be a problem with getting a grant from your education authority.

Qualifications can be gained through Youth Training, with practical experience and block or day-release courses. Trainees gain NVQs (National Vocational Qualifications) awarded by NEBAHAI (or NEB, the National Examinations Board for Agriculture, Horticulture and Allied Industries) and the National Proficiency Tests Council. The National Proficiency Tests are the only way agricultural workers can qualify for craftsman rates of pay under the Agricultural Wages Board (England and Wales).

National Vocational Qualifications
NVQs are awarded by bodies such as City and Guilds, BTEC and RSA. Each is made up of a number of units that set out standards that must be reached; a credit is awarded for each unit achieved. Trainees can select which units they do and train for them through TECs, companies, colleges, schools, universities and polytechnics; there are no entry requirements. Certificates show the unit credits gained. There are at present three NVQ levels (eventually there will be five), starting at Level 1.

NVQs currently available in land-based industries, awarded by the National Proficiency Tests Council, NEBAHAI, the Joint Council for Fish Husbandry and Gamekeeping and the Forestry Training Council are:

Level 1: Agriculture – foundation, poultry, animal care; commercial horticulture – amenity horticulture, crop production, mushroom production, garden centre operation; forestry – foundation; floristry.

Level 2: Agriculture – general livestock, general mechanised crop production, dairy, beef, goat, pig, sheep, estate maintenance; gamekeeping; floristry; poultry; commercial horticulture – fruit production, outdoor vegetable; nursery stock, protected cropping, mushroom production, garden centre operation, landscape maintenance, greenkeeping, sports turf, sports ground maintenance; arboriculture; hardlandscaping; forestry; fish husbandry.

Level 3: Floristry.

Further details from the National Council for Vocational Qualifications, 222 Euston Road, London NW1 2BZ.

NEBAHAI
The qualifications awarded by the National Examinations Board for Agriculture, Horticulture and Allied Industries are based on NVQs and include non-advanced one-year full-time college courses for National Certificate and Advanced National Certificate courses. Details of courses are available from Division II, City and Guilds of London Institute, 46 Britannia Street, London WC1X 9RG. Entrants to the NC courses should be at least 17 on 1

September of the year of entry, and may need to have one year of suitable practical experience and minimum academic qualifications (check with the college). Entrants to ANC courses need NC or equivalent qualifications and two years' experience (with one year following the NC course).

A full list of full-time and sandwich courses available in the UK up to postgraduate level is given in *Courses in Land-based Industries*, £9.95 from East Anglian Regional Advisory Council for Further Education, 2 Looms Lane, Bury St Edmunds, Suffolk IP33 1HE. For information about BTEC and degree courses, see Chapter 7.

Case Study

An Agricultural Apprentice discusses his job and training
Brian is at college working for the National Certificate in Agriculture.

I haven't got a farming background, but while I was at school I helped my cousin on his smallholding and found that I got more and more interested.

When I left school, I looked up farmers in the telephone book, and wrote to one at random asking for a job. He replied, and he took me on. It was an amazing piece of luck because he turned out to be a very caring person and keen for you to get on in life. He suggested that I should do an apprenticeship and he was always helpful. If there was anything I didn't understand, he would make sure that I went out working with someone who could show me. My mates at college say that I've been very lucky. So many employers seem to treat apprentices as cheap labour and don't bother to give them the instruction they need.

I worked on that farm for two-and-a-half years and I got plenty of experience. It was a 1,000-acre farm, mainly arable with a few beef stock, and very modern. We had all the latest machinery and even a computerised grain barn. I spent four days at work and the fifth in college. The college work was not difficult. In the morning we did theory and in the afternoon practical work, and it was so linked up with what I was doing on the farm that it was quite easy to grasp. For the first year it was mainly general agriculture, and in the second we went into the theory a bit more. A lot of it was to do with machinery – how it functions, how to care for it and how to correct faults.

My boss suggested that I should take up the option of spending my third year doing the full-time course for a National Certificate. I am still technically employed by him so I can return to him afterwards if I want to. I think the course is a good idea. I don't think the practical side is so marvellous, but that is probably because I had such good equipment on the farm. But the theory is useful and I want the qualification too.

There are things I miss in college. I miss the open life, being shut in a classroom for much of the day. And I find the regularity hard. There's no regularity in farming.

Farming is hard. My greatest disappointment was starting work in the middle of the harvest. You work from 5.30 am until 11.30 at night to get the corn in, not even stopping for lunch. My mates were out every evening and I missed the social life. But at other times the work is easier. In livestock farming, you can spread the workload, but in arable farming it comes in patches and you have to accept this. I don't find the cold weather as bad as some people – I don't take much notice of it. I just pile on the clothes and plod along.

If you want a fat pay packet you won't get it, but if you like an outdoor life and don't care too much about money, then farming is great. I would recommend it to anybody.

Agricultural Contracting

The shortage of tenant farms and the cost of buying land has led to the growth of agricultural contracting, and the business is expanding.

An agricultural contractor is someone who undertakes farm work on a contract basis and supplies the machinery, expertise and manpower to do the job. Contractors must be experienced and knowledgeable, because they receive no instructions except for a description of the job to be done and must decide on the most suitable methods themselves. The employer may be a private farmer, land agency or large land owner, such as a pension fund or investment company.

Many people set up in a small way with a tractor and a few implements and build up over the years to a large business, subcontracting work to others. This requires less capital initially than buying a farm and is therefore an attractive proposition. But it is not advisable to begin such a venture until you have considerable experience and are sure of the demand for your services, so some initial market research is needed. You must also not underestimate the skill involved in running a business. Anyone interested in this form of work would be best advised to begin as the employee of an already established contractor which may give only seasonal work to start with.

Working Conditions

Most contractors undertake general agricultural work and will take on all tasks from harrowing a field to the complete management of a farm. Others acquire a stock of machinery for specialist work and concentrate on a single activity such as drainage systems or treating of soil and crops from the air. The work can therefore range from employment in more conventional settings to highly specialised technical operations.

A contractor may need a yard and covered space for the machinery, and someone to help with taking messages, and with invoices and other office work.

Organisation

Contracting is now a recognised agricultural activity and has its own professional association: the National Association of Agricultural Contractors. The members work in a wide variety of operations, including land drainage, agricultural aviation, spraying and injection of fertiliser, general contracting, livestock management and staff recruitment and training. Aerial work includes crop spraying, fertiliser spreading and aerial photography. The Association expects members to provide an efficient service and to keep its codes of practice – they advise that a good reputation and reliability bring in business, but one job badly done can ruin it.

The Association provides access to cost-effective insurance schemes; status and recognition by potential customers; and the chance to gain ideas and share ideas through meeting other members.

For general inquiries, contact the Association at the address given in Chapter 8.

Case Study

An Agricultural Contractor talks about his work

My father was a farm manager so I think farming was in my blood. When I grew up, I didn't want to become a farm labourer but I couldn't afford my own farm, so I went in for engineering. After a few years in motor and aircraft engineering, I looked for a way to get started in agriculture and decided to set up as a contractor. That was over 25 years ago. I started alone, with a tractor, a plough and a pick-up baler. It was summer so I got harvesting jobs. My father was well-known in farming circles locally and that probably helped me, but I still had to prove my worth to customers. There was some reluctance to employ contractors because they had an image of unreliability and over-booking and I had to overcome this. It took a long time to establish mutual trust and confidence but I managed it. After two years, I took on a man to help me and today I have two depots and I employ 14 regular driver-operators, a general foreman, an engineer and two apprentices, as well as office staff.

We are general agricultural contractors and undertake all the routine farm jobs with the exception of land drainage. We have a nominal amount of complete farm management but mainly we contract to carry out specific tasks: silage making, seeding, haymaking, harvesting, and so on. We are busiest in the summer months, and from May until November I double the workforce by employing seasonal labour.

My engineering background has stood me in good stead for the mechanical aspect, which is what most contracting is about. The changeover from mixed farming to specialisation has meant that farmers have a need for skilled mechanised procedures to be carried out, and we are suppliers and operators of complex machinery.

I have one employee with a sound agricultural college background and he acts as our general agricultural adviser, but mainly I look for a mechanical bias plus some farming background when I employ staff. Training in agricultural machinery is a recommendation because my workers must be specialist machine operators – and better than the run of the mill.

Working for the Government

The Ministry of Agriculture, Fisheries and Food runs an advisory service, the Agricultural Development and Advisory Service (ADAS), for farmers and horticulturalists, staffed by regionally based teams of advisory officers. These officers form a bridge between the teaching and research establishments and the people involved in the practical application of new techniques in their working lives. They advise, not only on new methods, but on any difficulties and emergencies which may be encountered by farmers.

The Work of Advisory Officers

Advisory officers must be graduates or holders of suitable diplomas and be able to combine a knowledge of new research with an understanding of the practical aspects of farming. They must be able to liaise with the various agencies involved and, above all, get on well with the farmers for whom they are providing a service. The job entails a lot of travelling and is a mixture of outdoor and office work.

Experimental Farms

A more practical link is provided by the 11 experimental husbandry farms run by ADAS. These farms investigate and develop new ideas, conducting their research in a farming context. Compared with the total agricultural workforce they represent a very small area of employment but are worth describing because, for some people, they can provide the perfect balance between the academic atmosphere of a research job and the practical day-to-day working life. On an ADAS farm, you can always be sure of the practical value of your research.

Two ADAS agencies, the Farm and Countryside Service (with 1,800 professional and support staff) and the Field Research and Development Division (with 350 staff, half of them graduates or equivalent) are due to merge in April 1992. Recruitment in the professional and scientific grades is at graduate or equivalent level, with vacancies advertised in the national press and specialist journals, and interviews normally in early spring.

Senior Staff have an overall responsibility for the functioning of the farms and are specifically involved with determining and organising the experimental work.

Scientific Staff. Most graduate staff are employed as Advisory Officers, and most are recruited as graduates at Grade IV level, though there may be entry at Grade III for those with relevant experience. A good basic agricultural (or horticultural) training is essential, with the appropriate technical training for the chosen discipline. It is possible to transfer between disciplines, particularly from agriculture to husbandry or business management.

The minimum entry requirement for a Scientific Officer is HNC, but many entrants have an honours degree. The minimum requirement for an Assistant Scientific Officer is four GCSEs which must include maths or a science subject and English language. They see to the day-to-day running and recording of experiments and are involved with handling and collating data.

Farm Staff. The organisation of the practical aspects of the farms is dealt with by a farm manager who has a team of farm workers to carry out the necessary tasks. They are agricultural workers, like any others, but beyond this they must have an inquiring interest in what they are doing and be flexible in their working methods.

Conditions of Work
Experimental farms aim to demonstrate good husbandry techniques but the research and educational activities make the work very different from other types of farming. Animals and crops will often be raised in small experimental groups; occasionally work will be done in a way contrary to good commercial practice; and there will, of course, be no economic pressure to produce products. There will be less opportunity for mechanisation and the job will be complicated by the need for recording results.

The staffing ratio on an experimental farm is far higher than normal to cope with the additional work. A degree of coordination is required by everybody and people work very closely together. Loners will not easily fit in. There are also the public relations and educational functions of the farm to consider. Staff must be able to cope with open days, lectures, discussions, and be prepared to welcome large numbers of visitors to the farm.

Case Studies

An Agricultural Advisory Officer considers his duties
Mike is the deputy farm director of an experimental farm engaged in investigating aspects of upland farming. The farm is situated on the edge of moorland country and has a staff of 19 to run its 200 hectares.

After A levels I knew roughly that I wanted to do agricultural science. I had a loose connection with farming through an uncle, and before I went to university I worked for a time on an agricultural research station. That experience convinced me, so I went to Nottingham University where I hated the book work, but got by.

When I graduated I knew I didn't want to go into pure research so I looked for a job which would combine this with some practical farming experience. I took a post as a demonstrator on a university farm where the work was part academic and part farming. I did this for three years, during which I started a higher degree but didn't finish it. It taught me about basic research methods, but I felt that a lot of the research being done was not applicable to actual farming. I was more interested in developmental work (research in a farming context) so I applied to ADAS for direct entry into the advisory grades. A word of warning here for others like me: for direct entry you must be 26 and I was too young by a matter of months. I still had to wait. When I was accepted later, I asked particularly for work on an experimental farm. That was 12 years ago, and I've been in the work ever since.

Working on an experimental farm you get the opportunity to convince farmers of the importance of research. They can see the results in a way they can understand. On this farm we raise beef and sheep, and are particularly interested in problems of silage making and grazing in these upland conditions. We try to evolve good techniques and systems of farming, and are always thinking ahead. A large part of the work is passing our experience on. We have about 4,000 visitors a year, and that constitutes quite a lot of educational and public relations work. It is nice to be able to do this with no strings attached, which is why I prefer to work as a civil servant rather than for an industrial company.

A Farm Worker discusses his career to date
John has almost 35 years' experience of farm work behind him and remains enthusiastic about his job.

I'm not a country person, really. I came from near Heathrow Airport but I worked Saturdays on a farm as a boy, and our curate found me work on a farm in Devon. I worked for 13 years on very traditional farms, sometimes living in and sometimes in tied cottages, before I came here. After being beholden to one boss I found this farm very different. I was working with a lot of people for the first time and there was a general interest in what was going on, instead of just following a routine. It was a completely different world that I didn't know existed. The hours were better too. Now, I only work one weekend in three.

There is a lot of manual work setting up the projects: things like fencing. But the work is very varied and can involve travelling and meeting people. This year I went up to Smithfield Show with some of our cattle and I enjoyed that.

I've been here more than 20 years so I have seen the farm build up from small beginnings to what it is today. In the early days we started breeding pedigree Devons, but that fizzled out and then we went on to individual feeding programmes for 80 cattle. This meant a lot of weighing in and out, and timing of feeding. Now all this has got much more complicated and we may be using as many as 17 different kinds of silage at any one time.

Although this is an experimental farm, all the time I've been here I have never thought that anything we've done has been cruel. There are no calves in boxes, no keeping animals in the dark. Sometimes we do things we know will not work out. We have to accept this, though we farm workers sometimes try to influence the scientific staff who are producing the programmes. I'm always willing to argue!

Working for Industry

Large chemical companies, such as Fisons and ICI, employ research and advisory staff whose work is very similar to that of ADAS officers. The main difference is that these employees are subject to economic considerations, and the work they undertake must, to some extent, be in the firm's interests.

These companies also employ salesmen who demonstrate their products and advise clients on their use. This is a travelling job for which you need the ability to make easy contacts with people and have the confidence to speak with assurance on a number of subjects.

You will probably stand a better chance of such employment if you have taken a full-time college course. The practically based National Certificate in Agriculture may well be sufficient.

Salaries and Conditions of Work

Manual Workers
The basic wages of all workers involved in the production side of agriculture are laid down by the Agricultural Wages Board. The board recognises four levels of employment which are: (i) ordinary or unskilled, (ii) craftsman (for those who have successfully completed an apprenticeship or craft training scheme), (iii) appointment Grade II, supervisory (workers in charge of large numbers of animals or crops), and (iv) appointment Grade I, managerial (people with an overall management responsibility which includes controlling at least two full-time workers). Rates of pay for these grades are given below, and are the same for men and women.

	1991 weekly rates (men and women)			
Age	*Appointment Grade I*	*Appointment Grade II*	*Craftsman*	*Other Worker*
20+	£174.73	£161.79	£148.84	£129.43
19	–	–	£133.95	£110.66
18	–	–	£119.06	£ 98.37
17	–	–	–	£ 79.86
16	–	–	–	£ 67.56
15	–	–	–	£ 61.48

Non-employed status trainees in Youth Training receive a weekly training allowance of £29.50 during the first year, and in their second year, £35 weekly. Additional allowances may be paid for travel and lodging but the training allowance will be reduced. Employed agricultural trainees receive from £2.60 per hour.

The standard working week is 39 hours worked on five days, and overtime rates are paid for additional hours. Other benefits may include production bonuses, housing at a nominal rent, and, for single people, accommodation provided by the employer at a charge not above that fixed by the Agricultural Wages Board.

The annual paid holiday is two weeks, increasing to three after one year spent with the same employer. There is a statutory sick pay scheme, and employees are usually subject to the Government pension scheme unless their employer provides an alternative one.

Higher and Professional Grades
Managerial appointments within commercial agriculture usually have a substantial starting salary and an experienced manager should receive as much as managers shouldering comparable responsibilities in industry. Additionally, there are often profit-sharing or other incentive schemes.

Chapter 2

Horticulture

The word horticulture means, literally, garden culture but it is used today to describe a wide range of activities involving the raising of plants on a smaller scale than is practised in agriculture. A large part of horticultural activity is devoted to the provision and maintenance of plants for their beauty in parks and other open spaces. As most of this work is done in urban areas, it will be dealt with in Chapter 3, and this chapter will be concerned mainly with commercial horticulture.

Commercial Horticulture

Most of the fruit and vegetables which appear in greengrocers' shops are produced on holdings in the British Isles which can vary from vast, highly mechanised organisations to small family concerns. The large holdings are mainly concentrated in the eastern half of Britain, but there are exceptions to this rule. Another important part of the horticultural industry is the growing of garden plants, shrubs and cut flowers. Many different techniques are used in the cultivation of such a variety of produce, and conditions of work will vary according to the crop.

Working Conditions
Horticulturalists, like agricultural workers, are bound by the seasons and there will be busy times when essential tasks must be finished before a certain date and slacker ones when the pace will be slower. Apart from the type of plants raised, the main factors likely to affect working conditions are the size of the enterprise and its marketing arrangements.

On a large holding, mechanisation will remove many of the more routine jobs and will make the work more technical. Staff may also specialise in certain aspects of the firm's activities and this may or may not be to your advantage – some tasks are more interesting than others.

Most workers in small organisations need to be Jacks of all trades as work areas are often not clearly defined. The work will have variety, a reason why many people choose a life in horticulture. The plants themselves dictate this, as they have different needs at different times of the year.

Marketing techniques will also affect the variety of work. Many growers sell privately at their own gate, and may involve their workers in the business of selling. Others sell to wholesalers and produce must be graded, packed and labelled. In garden centres there will be a constant round of customers requiring expert advice and attention.

Qualities Required

A wide range of interests and abilities are required for working in horticulture. If you are mechanically minded, you may love driving a tractor around a large holding but if you like working with your hands you will probably be happier in a plant nursery or on a smaller, less mechanised holding.

Unless you are involved directly with the public, a life in horticulture can be a solitary one. Even if you are one of a large workforce, you will often find yourself working alone. The work is also physically hard. The summer is marvellous for those who work outside, but the winter is long and cold. And those people who spend their winters in warm greenhouses are still there in the summer when the sun streams through the glass and creates unwelcome heat and humidity. Every situation has its advantages and disadvantages. The greatest reward is the harvest of your labours. Whether carnations or sprouts, you will have made them grow.

Training and Qualifications

There are certain techniques every horticulturalist needs to know about, for example, the use of machinery, propagation methods and pest control. People who intend to assume responsibility will need a more in-depth knowledge of the theory behind current practices and, for management work, should receive some education in management and business techniques.

The training schemes are the same for horticulturalists as they are for agriculturalists, with the addition of a few courses specific to horticulture. Horticultural options are available in all the training schemes, and courses and information given in the preceding chapter apply equally to horticulture.

There are many part-time courses available, most of them leading to City and Guilds examinations Phases I (one-year course) and II (two years). The courses are taken by school leavers during Youth Training, and also by older people who do not need to have academic qualifications. Young people aged 16 to 18 can also take a full-time BTEC First Diploma course, followed by a National Diploma course. Those aged 18 or over who have just one or two good GCSEs can do the National Certificate in Horticulture (NCH) courses, followed by the Advanced National Certificate. Anyone gaining a credit or distinction in the NCH is able to go on an ND course.

For entry to an ND course at horticultural college, candidates must be aged 18 or over, with four GCSE subjects at grades A, B or C, which must be two of Group 1 (see below); one of Group 2 and one other.

Group 1: combined science, maths, chemistry, biology or rural biology, botany, zoology, geology, physics, physics with chemistry, integrated science, engineering science, and general/ agricultural/horticultural/rural or environmental science, or rural studies.

Group 2: English language, English literature, history, geography, economics, religious knowledge.

Anyone who has passed at least one A-level science subject (preferably biology) and studied another, or has an ND, can apply for a Higher National Diploma course. A list of horticultural colleges in England and Wales, with brief details of the courses they provide, is available from the Royal Horticultural Society.

The Horticultural Correspondence College, Freepost, Lacock, Chippenham, Wiltshire SN15 2BR, offers a course for the Royal Horticultural Society General Examination in Horticulture, which provides a nationally recognised qualification for people starting in horticulture and for amateur gardeners; study courses for the exam are also offered at evening classes in some further education colleges and at agricultural colleges (a list is available from the RHS).

An Open Learning Unit at Capel Manor College, Bullsmoor Lane, Enfield, Middlesex EN1 4RQ, covers certain specific aspects of horticulture; there is no Open University course.

The traditionally prestigious qualification for horticulturalists is awarded by the Royal Horticultural Society. Originally known as the National Diploma in Horticulture, it is titled the Master of Horticulture (RHS) award. For details write to the Royal Horticultural Society's Garden, Wisley, Woking, Surrey GU23 6QB.

Another sought-after award is the Kew Diploma which can be obtained after three years' full-time commitment, divided between study and garden work at Kew. The course is geaared to amenity horticulture and covers, very comprehensively, scientific, technical and managerial subjects within this activity at first degree level. Students spend a third of their time in academic study and the remainder as working gardeners in the Royal Botanic Gardens. In recognition of their work on the upkeep of the gardens, they are paid a subsistence allowance which does away with the need for a grant.

To be eligible for the course, intending students must have worked in horticulture for at least two years with training to NEB Level 2 (or equivalent) and be aged between 18 and 26. They should have at least three GCSE passes (or equivalent) and one science at GCE A level.

Young people studying for A levels can apply as sixth-form entry candidates for the Kew Diploma, but will need to do a year's practical work before starting the course, and would do a further 12 months outside Kew after the first year of the course. Details from the School of Horticulture, Royal Botanic Gardens, Kew, Richmond, Surrey TW9 3AB.

Competition is strong. Each year between 200 and 300 applications are received, and 20 students are admitted to the course. Successful students can expect to find employment in positions of responsibility in a variety of horticultural settings, and the Kew Diploma is particularly respected abroad.

There is a similar course for the Diploma of Horticulture, Edinburgh, at the Royal Botanic Garden. The three-year course in practical and theoretical training in amenity and ornamental horticulture is recognised as a first degree equivalent. Further details from the Department of Horticultural Training, Royal Botanic Garden, Edinburgh EH3 5LR.

Qualifications needed for a university degree course in horticulture are three A-level science subjects; the courses are available at the universities of Reading, Nottingham, London (Wye College, Ashford, Kent) and Strathclyde.

At present graduates in horticulture are not as well placed for getting a job as those with more practical experience and lower qualifications. In future, degree courses may become sandwich type, including practical experience. A new BSc degree course in horticulture at Writtle College, Chelmsford, Essex encourages applicants to gain experience before entry, though there is no direct stipulation of a practical pre-entry year.

Postgraduate courses are taken by those who have a first degree in horticulture or BSc in a science subject such as biology, botany, chemistry or physics.

Case study

A Kew Student talks about the course
David is in his second year of study for the Kew Diploma.

My interest in horticulture started in my own garden where I worked every weekend. I left school when I was 16 and took a job as a gardener for a local authority for two-and-a-half years. During this time I took day-release classes and took my City and Guilds examinations. Then I applied for the Kew course, but I was turned down, so I wrote asking for an ordinary gardening job. I got it and I worked for a further two years in different parts of the gardens. I also took A levels in horticultural science and botany at night school. Then I applied again, and this time I was accepted.

The scope here is tremendous. There's everything you could possibly be interested in – so much, in fact, that you have to make a choice. I'm particularly keen on trees and shrubs, which is why botanic gardens work appealed to me. You work with such a variety of species. It has its dangers, though. Last year I fell out of a tree and broke my back in two places. I was laid up for six months, and had to repeat a year of the course, but it hasn't put me off!

The academic side is tough. There are seven graduates on the course at present and *they* find it difficult. I have to work very hard. We are given projects to complete and they are like small theses. There are times when you think you can't get away from the place. You have to work weekends too, because that is the only time the Herbarium Library is open.

Before you start the course you come here looking young and fresh-faced and you finish looking haggard and old! – No, seriously, you come out much more mature. And the qualification stands you in good stead – especially if, like me, you are interested in working abroad.

Employment Opportunities in Horticulture

A talk with the Personnel Officer of a large, well-established company

We have three main areas of activity: growing houseplants, raising hardy stock and landscaping. We are a friendly firm, and many of our employees stay with us for a long time. We like to promote people we know.

When we appoint young people, we look for basic skills but not necessarily academic ability. During the first couple of years, they usually find their own level and, by then, we know if they will be useful to us. They must be hard-working and reliable as well as horticulturally gifted. We try to encourage the most promising people by finding them a supervisory post after about three years and, for those with academic ability, we suggest a year in college.

We have our own fairly structured career ladder, from craft workers through supervisory posts to managerial grades, but we don't relate qualifications to these grades. We do not insist, for instance, that our higher office staff have HNDs or degrees. We prefer to go on our own assessment of their abilities.

There is a problem with all positions of responsibility in that they involve handling people. How do you encourage and control your workers? We run our own in-service courses, but we also make use of local ATB short courses on instructional and management techniques, and sometimes we send people to training sessions run by the Royal Agricultural Society at Kenilworth in Warwickshire.

We encourage people to gain as wide an experience as possible, and sponsor them on exchanges abroad. We also have a hostel for single employees and a number of houses which we rent to senior staff. I think we are very paternalistic but it pays off. We want to keep our good employees because they are our future.

Working in Outdoor Vegetable, Bulb and Flower Production

Many of these crops are grown on a large scale, by specialist growers using highly mechanised techniques. This is particularly so in the eastern half of England. Elsewhere, holdings tend to be smaller and crops will be concentrated where the soil suits them.

Outdoor vegetable, bulb and flower production is the backbone of the horticultural industry, and there will always be a demand for workers in the area. Large firms may offer more scope in terms of a career ladder as they will probably have a structure of supervisory and managerial posts through which you can progress, but the work may have less variety as employees will tend to specialise in certain aspects only.

In many ways, conditions are similar to those of arable farming. Tractor-driving will be a common activity and there will be a range of implements to manipulate. Main tasks will be ploughing, seed bed preparation, planting, pest control and, finally, harvesting. There is always a certain amount of hard work, especially in flower production, and all produce has to be graded and packed for marketing.

Working in a Plant Nursery or Garden Centre

A plant nursery is a place where plants are propagated and raised to a state in which they can be sold for permanent planting. A garden centre is a place in which these plants are sold. Sometimes nurseries and garden centres are run as one operation – on the same site; sometimes they are separate.

Some nurseries specialise in one particular plant, for instance, roses, azaleas or clematis, and use techniques of propagation built up over years of experience. They usually sell by mail order or supply garden centres on request. Working in such places can be fascinating for the enthusiast, dedicated to the plant in question, but the availability of jobs will depend on where you live. Roses, for instance, thrive on East Anglian soil, and you will have to discover what is grown in your area by inquiring locally.

Many garden centres, especially those in urban areas, do not have enough land to grow their own plants on site, and staff in these places will be involved mainly with the care of container-grown plants in stock and with the business of selling them. To carry out this work, you will need a good practical knowledge of the plants you are selling, as many customers will seek your advice about the suitability and habits of the varieties in which they are interested.

Nursery and garden centre work is the least mechanised of all jobs in commercial horticulture. It is a job for plant enthusiasts, offering scope to raise plants from tiny seedlings or cuttings, and often to work with a variety of plants. Propagation is a skilled job and is fascinating and rewarding. So is pruning, but there are also the routine tasks such as watering, preparing soil, spraying with insecticide, and general nursery maintenance. All are equally important. One advantage of this work over other horticultural jobs is the mixture of inside and outside tasks. On the very worst days, it is often (though not always) possible to escape to a warm greenhouse, and everyone who has worked outside in the freezing rain will know the value of that.

Case Studies

Miss A: A Nursery and Garden Centre Owner

I trained under one of the old school: a head gardener who wore a green baize apron and required all of us to wash our tools every night before we stopped work. I learnt a whole range of disciplined procedures from him which I still practise myself, and a little of this rubs off on the nursery here. But often, these things are niceties which you can't afford today.

I have had this nursery for 25 years. It is a smallholding of three acres and we combine the two functions of growing and selling to the public. I don't think we are very typical. For a start, many small nurseries are family concerns, run by members of a family, whereas I am alone and employ four staff. I also think it is unusual to offer the range of plants we do on a plot of this size. We are completely independent and grow most of the plants ourselves. I do some buying in, but there is not much profit in this if you operate on a small scale. We buy in mainly because of geographical limitations or the need for specialist care which we cannot provide. It is difficult to raise roses in this part of the country, and plants such as rhododendrons and azaleas have now become a specialist field. We will also buy in to meet an unusual request, because we pride ourselves in being able to offer a complete range of plants.

Nursery work is very intensive. Every inch of our land is used for something. With small-scale mixed cultivation, there is no place for mechanisation, and I like it this way. I am not totally guided by commercial considerations, either. We are quite prepared to grow uncommercial plants because we are enthusiasts. There's no big money to be made in small-scale nursery work, anyway. You have to want to do it, and be prepared for the realities. It's always too hot, too cold, too wet or too something – but you must work on. Occasionally, people get the idea that you put in a few cuttings and that they strike and that's the whole story. But it's definitely not. You have to plan two or three years ahead, and if you sell direct to the public, as we do, you can never predict exactly what the demand will be. This means some wastage and, sometimes, unexpectedly large orders that are difficult to meet.

When I employ staff, I look for keenness rather than college training. College people tend to lack a practical attitude and not know about economics. None of us are trained in that sense but we all need a lot of knowledge. Every plant has different habits, different propagation needs and so forth. We have all learned on the job.

Stuart: Nursery and Garden Centre Worker

I was born in the country and we always grew our own vegetables. I discovered I had a flair for plants. I can do something to a plant to make it grow better.

When I left school, I worked for a time in a horticultural shop, and then I was offered the job here. In the shop I dealt with the advisory side (what chemicals to use to cope with the various problems) and that knowledge was useful when I came here. But this is what I wanted to do, to be working directly with plants.

I like the contact with people too. Sometimes they interrupt you when you are involved with something you really want to continue with, but I can always manage to come up with a smile. I think if you like plants, you like people, and selling to people is what it's all about. That's when I think I'm earning my money – when I break away from something I'm enjoying doing to talk to someone who's a right bore!

I think everyone enjoys doing what they're good at, and I know I can do this. I enjoy the outdoor life too, and the fact that you are always learning. But you have to be dedicated, and be prepared to stick at it. It is a lifetime's job. I did no training in a formal way, but I would advise young people to get some qualifications. Most employers ask for them, especially for the better jobs, and wages can be higher if you are qualified.

Working in a Glasshouse

Glasshouse work is probably the least physically demanding and most technical of all horticultural activities. You will spend most of your time inside, in a controlled environment, and the most you will have to endure is perhaps a little too much heat and humidity in the summer. But you will be responsible for all the needs of your crop, and this has become a highly technical procedure.

Crops commonly grown under glass include salad vegetables, flowers, and ornamental and tender plants. In the artificial atmosphere of a greenhouse it is possible to be independent of the seasons, but plants still have their cycle of growth, and demand for exotic varieties will be high at certain times of the year: for example at Christmas time, and on Mothering Sunday. This will mean that you, as well as other horticultural workers, must be able to sustain an uneven working pace. In larger nurseries, almost all the monotonous tasks will be mechanised, and you will be left with work such as propagation, potting and generally monitoring the progress of the crop. But all systems sometimes break down, and you must be ready to carry out tasks manually when this happens. You must also know exactly what plants need in terms of ventilation, heating, irrigation and feeding, so that automatic systems can be correctly set.

As in other areas of work, conditions will vary according to the extent of the mechanisation. Some glasshouse nurseries still depend almost entirely on the manual skill and management of the workforce; others have whole empires of vegetables and flowers under glass, with computers controlling the entire operation.

Case Study

A Horticultural Apprentice talks about his training
David is in the third year of his training and works for a large company producing house-plants under glass.

I used to do the garden at home and flog the produce to my Dad who had a greengrocer's shop. After school I wanted to carry it on, so I applied to two or three nurseries and garden centres. I chose this firm because it has an international reputation and runs a number of nurseries producing different kinds of plants. The opportunities to diversify appealed to me.

I got seven good grades, so people at school were a bit shocked that I wanted to leave and go in for horticulture. It's not renowned for being a brainy occupation. But I think that is a misconception nowadays. There is more and more technical work involved as larger nurseries are becoming automated. In greenhouse work, a computer can run the whole thing at the flick of a switch and you can get involved with the business of programming and managing equipment.

This nursery has 30 plants under glass, all producing house-plants. Each group of plants needs different treatment, and we apprentices rotate around the blocks to get experience of them all. I'm working in the hydroculture unit at the moment. This involves a fairly new technique of transferring soil plants into clay aggregate and feeding them a liquid solution. Once they are established in the new medium, it is impossible to overfeed them. They just absorb as much as they need, so it makes them very easy to manage in the home. The block is mechanised but not computerised, and I think I like that balance. The boring, backbreaking tasks are taken away, but you look after the plants yourself because you control the switches. There are plenty of manual jobs left. Yesterday, for instance, I spent the morning putting shading in a glasshouse and the afternoon damping down plants and then doing some potting and spraying. For most routine jobs we get piecework rates so that adds an incentive.

On my training scheme, we do five separate block weeks in college each year and, pretty generally, that covers the stuff I don't get here – cut flowers, salad vegetables and so on. The theory side deals with soils, pests and diseases. We also work for the City and Guilds exams and take Proficiency Tests.

In greenhouse work you spend 98 per cent of your time inside. It's quiet and spacious, and the plants look beautiful. I'm very interested in hydroculture at the moment but I'm still undecided about what I'll end up doing. I'd like to go abroad for a while and I know that, with my apprenticeship behind me, I can always study later if I feel like it. I think it's a mistake to specialise too early. I want a wide view now and I'm keeping my options open.

Fruit Farming

Two main groups of fruit are grown in the British Isles: tree fruit (that is, apples, pears, plums and cherries), and soft fruit (that is, strawberries, raspberries, blackcurrants etc). Tree fruit cultivation is mainly limited to the southern half of England, but soft fruit production is widespread, even extending into parts of Scotland.

Fruit farming is an almost totally outside job with two busy seasons: pruning in the winter and harvesting in the summer and autumn. At other times, the work is similar to many other agricultural and horticultural jobs, consisting of preparing the soil, planting, and pest and weed control. Mechanisation, especially in soft fruit production, may be fairly advanced in fruit farming, and new technology for increasing production and more efficient storage is being introduced all the time.

Case Studies

A Fruit Farmer outlines his work
Richard grows dessert apples on 12 acres of hilly land, and markets the crop himself.

I'm conservation minded and I think that most growers use too much fertiliser and too much spray. I use half the recommended amount and I get satisfactory results. If you use a lot of fertiliser you get blown-up and tasteless apples – and I hate to think what insecticides do to wildlife. Unfortunately you can't do without them, but I find that I can minimise their effects by using them sparingly and spraying in the late evening. I also have my own methods of storage. Cold storage has a bad effect on the taste of fruit, to my mind, and I barn-store mine.

I came here 16 years ago after doing a general agricultural course at a farm institute, and working on a number of fruit farms and in a plant nursery. It is sensible to get a range of experience before setting up on your own. I learnt a lot from mine.

Growing apples is a waiting game. Generally, they don't do anything for about seven years. Initially, many people plant soft fruit, which matures more quickly, between the rows of apple trees to make the farm economic during this time. Currently, I'm branching out into bees. They fit in well on a fruit farm as they help with pollination. I also hire mine out to neighbouring farmers for this purpose. I'm paid so much for each hive.

My busiest time of the year is winter, when I'm pruning. It has to be done by a certain time and there is nothing for it but to keep going until I've finished. I'm on the verge of needing permanent help, but would have to grow quite a lot more to justify the help financially. From the end of August until the end of October I employ 12 to 14 people for picking and grading, and I find this casual labour no trouble. They work quickly and efficiently and I work alongside them, which I think they like.

I can't stand wholesalers. They bark all the time, push you down to rock bottom prices, and make 100 per cent profit for themselves. So I do all my own marketing and I enjoy it. There is a psychology of selling which makes it an interesting exercise. I sell virtually everything (30 tons of apples a year) from the gate here through extensive advertising. I always use gimmicks: phrases like 'Well worth finding' to make my advertisements different from the rest, and I display the apples in large trays at the gate. I sell them in 30lb boxes and find that people are quite ready to buy this quantity rather than 5lb bags.

It's a very congenial life and much less of a tie than raising livestock. I couldn't stand working indoors.

Fred, a Fruit Farm Worker, talks about work on the farm.

I've worked on a few farms, both large and small, and there's little difference, really. On a small farm, you work with your employer doing a bit of everything and get to know the running of the place, but you're not involved with the business side of things. On a large farm, it's more mechanised and you have company, which can be nice, but even on a 100-acre farm you can spend a lot of time alone. It's quite a lonely existence, wherever you work.

You have to keep to the seasons. Pruning is the hardest job during cold winter days. It's rather like an endurance test. You get into a rhythm. It's up to you where you cut, and sometimes it can be quite soothing. There is a lot of tractor driving (cutting grass, spraying fruit, gathering in the crop) and there's the interest of having the casual workers in for picking.

It's smashing in the summer – very occasionally like being in the South of France with gorgeous weather and the apple blossom around you! You see the season through and then there is harvesting, and back again to the winter cold.

If it were spring and summer all the time I'd have no reservations, but the winter is so long. Compared to general agriculture, fruit farming is all outside. Even so, as soon as the sun shines, it's all worth it.

Working for the Government and Industry

ADAS employs horticultural as well as agricultural officers, specialising in bulbs, field vegetables, fruit, glasshouses and protected crops and hardy ornamental nursery stock. The section on ADAS in Chapter 1 (see p 18) gives an idea of the work of horticultural officers which has identical aims and differs only in the specialist operations carried out.

Industry, too, employs horticulturalists for research and advisory work.

Gardening for Private Employers

There are still a few private estates which employ gardeners for general, small-scale work. The conditions offered are too varied to generalise about. If you see yourself as a spade-in-hand gardener, working with a variety of plants, you may wish to look for this kind of work, but you must be careful to clarify your position with your employer before you begin work. You could become a dogsbody, or you could find yourself in a pleasant haven, doing a rewarding job. There are no rules for finding this kind of work. Jobcentres, local papers, or even local gossip are the most likely sources of information.

For the price of a few tools it is also possible to be your own boss and help people in their gardens. But you must be sure of getting your custom, and you must know what you are doing. No one will ask you again if you pull up a rare plant with the weeds!

Rates of Pay

Wages for horticultural workers are set by the Agricultural Wages Board and are identical to those of agricultural workers given on p 22. People in managerial positions can also expect similar levels of remuneration.

Chapter 3
Outdoor Work in Towns and Cities

This chapter outlines the opportunities for people living in towns and cities interested in gardening or who want to work outdoors. All urban areas have their garden centres and nurseries, usually situated in the suburbs, where conditions of work will be very similar to those described in the previous chapter. But the main employer in all built-up areas is local government. All local councils have Parks and Recreation departments (sometimes called Leisure and Amenities) which look after the open spaces and promote leisure and sporting activities in their area. Within these departments there is a considerable range of employment at all levels of responsibility.

Conditions of Work in Local Government

The main advantages of working for local government are that conditions of work are clearly laid down and jobs are usually secure. There is a set career structure and on-the-job training opportunities are good. This means that it is possible to begin work as an untrained school leaver, and progress up the ranks to a supervisory position by experience on the job and taking day- or block-release courses.

The emphasis on amenities in parks has changed over the years from providing attractive open spaces, to creating activity areas. However, the aesthetic element still remains. Parks are laid out with an eye on the effect of their flower-beds, shrubberies and trees. But they are also very much thought of as play spaces for young children and, space permitting, sporting and recreational areas for older people. This means that the jobs available can be divided into two groups – those concerned primarily with aspects of gardening and those dealing with the people who use the parks.

Amenity Horticulture

Gardening in parks and other public places is known as amenity horticulture. Although much of the necessary knowledge is of a general horticultural nature, the work is characterised by being directed towards providing a public service, rather than towards running a commercial enterprise.

Amenity horticulture is the main activity on which the career structure of outdoor work in local government is based. Most of the work is concerned with the maintenance of parks, but it also includes looking after sports fields, the areas around public buildings, roadside verges and roundabouts. There are three main levels of employment: craft, technical and professional. These represent a progression from the gardener through the supervisory grades to the managerial and executive staff at the top levels.

Craftsmen

At all levels of the craftsman grade the work will be concerned with gardening, and will keep you out in the open air. Much of the work will, necessarily, be routine – grass must be cut, borders weeded, paths swept – but for everyone above assistant gardener grade, knowledge of plants will be needed. You must know how and when to prune roses and shrubs, when to use fertilisers, how bedding plants are laid out and how to carry out a whole range of specialised tasks, including the maintenance of machinery. Although most jobs involve general gardening in the parks, there are opportunities to specialise in nursery work, arboriculture (which is the care of trees), and sports groundsmanship.

Training

It is possible to spend your life as an unskilled gardener, but the work will ultimately be more rewarding if you take advantage of the training schemes on offer. There are two ways of doing this. You can take part straight from school when you are 16, in which case your employer will be obliged to provide on-the-job training and send you for day-release college education. Or you can apply for a job as an assistant gardener in the hope that you will be given the opportunity to attend a day-release course at some time. Some applicants may be accepted after Youth Training. In either case, your employer will need to be convinced that you can cope with the college course. This does not mean that you have to be very academic. A lot of the college work involves the learning of practical skills. But you must have plenty of common sense, be able to remember the information you are taught, and your English must be good enough to deal with the theory work. Some local authorities prefer their gardeners to have a few GCSEs in subjects such as botany, environmental studies, English or maths; others give intelligence tests and make their decisions based on the results of these tests.

Day-release courses prepare you for the City and Guilds examinations, Phases I and II. These courses are backed up by on-the-job training, which is a continuous process in the early years of employment. Some authorities organise their own structured training schemes. (Islington Council offers job training in gardening and horticulture, specialising in nursery work, grounds tendering, tree maintenance or parks and playing fields, with block-release courses at a local college to study for internal horticultural exams, City and Guilds certificates and NVQs.)

Once you have become a chargehand, which is what you become when you reach the top of the craftsman grades, there are opportunities to progress to a technical or supervisory position by taking further training. This usually takes the form of a year spent at one of the horticultural training establishments.

Life as a Gardener
Working in amenity horticulture means that you are not dependent upon commercial production or actual hours of work to earn your money. So tasks can be organised to take account of bad weather, and you will not have to work outside in pouring rain unless a job is particularly urgent.

Sometimes gardeners work in 'gangs', having responsibility for a group of small parks, and operating from a home base which provides some indoor comforts. Gardening gangs appear to be very happy and companionable groups, with each member contributing what he or she can and, where necessary, supporting others in the gang. Sometimes they work alone, and are responsible for a small garden where there is a hut to provide shelter. You will know which type of job you would prefer. Most employers will be sympathetic to your wishes and will try to fit you in where you would be happiest.

There are four levels of gardener craftsman: Grade 1, trainee; Grade 2, assistant gardener; Grade 3, gardener, and Grade 4, chargehand. Apart from trainees, for whom there are separate arrangements people in these positions will be paid on grades 1 to 5 of the local government salary scales. The chargehand will have responsibility for the day-to-day organisation of the work and will be directly responsible to the area supervisor who makes decisions about the long-term care of the park.

Case Study

A Municipal Parks Gardening Gang
I talked to George, the chargehand, Brian and Ian, assistant gardeners, and Sarah, aged 16, who is a trainee.

George

I've always liked gardening. I started off with my uncle's garden when I was a boy. I enjoyed helping him and learning the names of the plants. When I left school, the careers people told me I couldn't be a gardener in Central London, so I found my own job as a trainee nurseryman at a garden centre. I did that for a year, but the pay was only £18 a week (that was 10 years ago) and it really wasn't enough. So I started working in Woolworth for three times the money. I didn't like it a bit. It was so closed in and dark and dingy. In the meantime I found that, after the age of 18, I could join the Council as an assistant gardener and it didn't matter that I had no O levels. So I joined on my 18th birthday.

I have been here for seven years now and, as the Chargehand, I organise the work of our gang. I am going to college on day-release for my City and Guilds Phase II exam and I find that interesting. It widens your ideas, talking to other people and hearing what they do. When gardening, it is very much a matter of opinion when you should do things and what methods you should use, so it is good to exchange ideas with other people.

I like my job very much and wouldn't think of leaving it. But I would like to broaden my experience, especially in general landscaping. I'd like to travel around a bit – to go abroad and see some of our exotic plants in their natural environment.

Sarah

I like being out in the open. I didn't know anything about gardening before I came here, but now I am enjoying it very much. My mum saw an advertisement in the local paper, and suggested that I try for it. I had an interview, and an IQ test, and then I was accepted. My first job was picking all the heads off the geraniums (dead heading, it's called) and after that I did lots of weeding. I hate weeding but I like everything else.

In my first year I will have to do some time in all the parks departments. I think I will like the nursery, but I am not looking forward to the arboriculture because I don't like climbing trees! Next year I will go to college on day-release.

Brian

I took the job so that I would be working outside. I'd had enough of indoor work. I had thought of doing a course in Building Trades, but I thought this might be better, and now I am here I am pleased with that decision. The relations in our gang are good. Sometimes we work together and sometimes in pairs, sometimes even alone. Mostly, though, it's a very companionable way of working.

Ian

I just liked being outside. I used to mow tennis courts, but this is better. There's more variety in the work.

Working in the Nursery of a Parks Department

Nurseries are at the hub of any parks department as they produce the plants and shrubs which appear in public gardens each year. The work is largely concerned with propagating plants from seeds and cuttings, and raising them to the point when they are ready to be planted out. This means that this is an excellent job for plant lovers. Most of the work involves skilled horticultural tasks. There is a minimum of routine maintenance, though as most nurseries aim to be self-supporting to save money, you have to be versatile and be able to turn your hand to such jobs as glazing broken greenhouses and constructing cold frames.

Case Studies

Vic, a Nursery Manager

My family used to have a farm, but then we moved into London and I chose nursery work as the next best thing. I still think it was the best choice I could have made.

You sow some seeds, and then at the end of a certain period, you have plants – all because of you. That's what the job is about.

Here at the nursery we work both inside and outside. So when the weather is bad we have the luxury of being able to work in a heated greenhouse. We also have no dealings with the public, which I like. It cuts down on the 'aggro' and we can get on with the job. We raise about a quarter of a million plants a year, so we are always busy.

We don't discriminate between our workers on the grounds of their grades. We all do a bit of everything, though I, as manager, have to plan the budget. Since cuts were introduced, we have had to make economies, but I have found ways of doing this without affecting the workforce. We've saved £500 on oil in three months by insulating and repairing the greenhouses, and a further £1,000 a year by changing from terra cotta to disposable pots. If we went over our budget, the Council might start cutting down on our staff and we don't want that. In fact, the worst aspect of the money shortage, from our point of view, is that we cannot recruit and train as many young people as we would like. We have a lad here at the moment on a YOPS* (Youth Opportunities) scheme, and there is work here for more – if only the money was available.

I've worked in several nurseries and this is by far the best because of the staff. I've gathered them up from other nurseries and they are my choice. So we all work well together. I have been manager here for 12 years now – too long, I suppose. But the next grade up would take me into office work and that's something I don't want.

David, a Chargehand

You are away from it all here. You wouldn't know you were in London, and I like that. When I was at school I was interested in gardening, and I have worked in nurseries ever since. I took the Local Government Training Board certificate in amenity horticulture, which meant day-release classes for three years, and now I've been at this nursery for six years.

I like nursery work because there is more real gardening than in the parks. We are mainly involved with producing plants and I get a lot of satisfaction from seeing them grow. Most of the work is potting up, pricking out seedlings, taking cuttings and preparing bedding plants. We have the general clearing, weeding, spraying and watering as well (watering can be an endless task) but that seems a minor part of the work. We also get the opportunity to grow our own plants. There are some orchids in one greenhouse, and someone is growing some stagshorn ferns.

When I first came here, we only did bedding and decorative plants, but now we produce shrubs and trees too. We also do floral decoration when it is required for special events in the borough. There is a lot of work, and it's very varied so you never get bored. Time flies and you seem to get home quickly!

We do have some shift work. I work every other weekend. But that is more than made up for by the happy working atmosphere. We are a small group – just seven of us – and that gives us a closeness so that we all work together like one big happy family, really. It is a very relaxed job.

Specialist Work in Amenity Horticulture

Arboriculture is the culture and maintenance of trees for their beauty and amenity value. Most parks departments have a tree gang, which is a team of workers who care for the trees in all

* Now YT (Youth Training).

public places in a particular area. They need to know about raising and planting young trees, and caring for them in their maturity by pruning and eradicating any diseases.

A 10-week course in tree surgery for craftsmen covers safety as well as basic skills, at Merrist Wood College of Agriculture and Horticulture in Surrey. National Certificate courses in arboriculture are also offered at Merrist Wood, as well as at Otley College, Suffolk; Lancashire College of Agriculture and Horticulture and Lincolnshire College of Agriculture and Horticulture. National Diploma courses in arboriculture are available at Merrist Wood and at Askham Bryan College, North Yorkshire, which also has an ND course specialising in urban forestry.

In Scotland there are NC courses in arboriculture at Clinterty Agricultural College, Aberdeen and Elmwood Agricultural College, Fife. Some universities include arboriculture in their forestry courses. The Royal Forestry Society has introduced a further qualification, the Certificate and National Diploma in Arboriculture. For details, see Part 2. As well as working for local government, arboriculturalists are employed by woodland contractors, and the larger landscape and garden centres which provide such services to their customers. Well-qualified people may also find work in an advisory capacity.

Groundsmanship is concerned with the maintenance of soil and grass, or turf, especially for sporting activities. Each sport has its own exacting requirements, so different techniques must be used. As well as the parks or leisure and recreation departments of local authorities, employers include private sports clubs, including growing numbers of golf clubs, and other institutions that provide sporting facilities, such as schools, universities and hotels. There are also some private contractors.

Basic experience of this work is acquired by every trainee in amenity horticulture, but established groundsmen who wish to gain further qualifications can do so by taking the examinations of the Institute of Groundsmanship, to whom inquiries can be made (see Part 2, p 109). Some agricultural colleges run specialist options in turf culture and groundsmanship and these are listed in Part 2.

Floristry is not primarily an outdoor job but has its roots in amenity horticulture as it concerns floral decoration. The florist must not only have an eye for arrangement but must know about the habits and characteristics of many different plants – what their cut life is, at what stage to cut them and how to cut correctly for different purposes. The techniques used for making bouquets must also be learnt.

Most people enter their first job as an unskilled worker and learn either on the job or through a City and Guilds day-release course. Several agricultural colleges run one-year full-time, or longer sandwich courses in floristry. They are listed in *Courses in Land-based Industries*.

Some local authorities employ florists, but the main source of work is probably with contracting companies and interior landscape firms who undertake large-scale floral decorations for special events, industry, commerce and public buildings. The girl so beautifully surrounded by flowers in your local florist's shop is probably functioning only as a shop assistant, with the skilled work being undertaken by her boss, the owner. This may not always be the case, however, so local inquiries might be worthwhile.

Supervisory and Managerial Work

Supervisors are the technical assistants who are responsible for the activities of the manual staff and the day-to-day running of the parks in their area. Some may specialise in areas such as landscape design, and all function to some extent in an advisory capacity. They have varied opportunities for creative horticultural planning, according to the attitude of their superiors. Although they are office-based, the greater proportion of their time is spent in the parks.

Training and Qualifications
All supervisors must be experienced practical horticulturalists, and must also have organising ability. In the past, it was usual for the more able chargehands to progress to the supervisory grades, but this is less common today. This is perhaps because chargehands tend to gain their experience in a limited area, and the job is more effectively done by people whose perspectives are wider. The most usual qualifications for supervisory work are a BTEC ND in amenity horticulture or HND in horticulture.

Case Study
Robin, a Parks Supervisor
Robin is one of four area supervisors in a city parks department.

> I would be fulfilled as a working gardener, but I cannot afford it. If
> the National Trust were to offer me a good wage to be head gardener

somewhere, I would go like a shot. But good money only comes with the kind of job I'm doing here.

Originally, I did a hotel management course, mainly because my dad kept a pub, and it seemed a sensible thing to do. I worked in hotels for three or four years, and hated it. I used to have dinner with the other managers (eating steak tartare when I would have preferred fish and chips) and they all had problems – drink problems, marriage problems, gambling problems, etc. It was an awful world and I had to get out. I was inside for days on end and never felt the fresh air.

I made the decision that I wanted to work in the open and I first tried to become a landscape architect. It seemed attractive. Landscape architects spend most of the time outside and are not involved with management. So I did an evening course at a polytechnic while I was still working at something else all day, but it was too much. I had none of the background knowledge and I just could not make it. However, I did gain an interest in plant material, so I decided to become a horticulturalist and went to agricultural college for an OND course in amenity horticulture. I wanted to be a practical horticulturalist, not a management man.

After I qualified, I went to Edinburgh to work in the Botanical Garden as an assistant gardener, hoping to attend some of the lectures there as well. By this time I was 28, and my take-home pay was still a pittance. It was just not possible to survive. So I got a job as a landscape foreman with a local authority. I didn't want to do this. I didn't want to push men around. I wanted to work with plants, but I needed the higher pay.

In the post I have now, my role is to manage the labour force and see that the day-to-day running of the gardens in my area goes according to plan. I spend about 15 per cent of my time in the office on routine paperwork. The rest of the time I am outside. But there is too much dull supervision – checking that the benches are clean, making sure the litter has been picked up – and not enough horticultural work, especially in the winter months. That is the trouble with parks departments. A lot of the work is clearing up after the public. The other day I spent the morning pruning shrubs, simply because I enjoy it. But really, that is the gardeners' work.

On the bonus side, I have a boss who is sympathetic to people doing their own thing. I am still interested in being a landscape designer, and he has let me have charge of the replanting of a whole garden this winter. I found that exciting. I've also chosen about £1,000-worth of plants to go in other parks and I take the opportunity to co-operate with the nursery staff in deciding what plants they will raise. It is much more interesting than simply accepting what comes and planting it mindlessly, wherever there happens to be a space. That is all I am required to do, but I suppose I have extended my job to give myself more satisfaction.

Managerial Staff. All parks departments are headed by a parks superintendent who usually has officer assistants. The superintendent is responsible for the overall planning and running of the authority's parks and will be involved in dealing with conflicting interests, deciding on policies, allocating money and putting the department's viewpoints across to the politicians.

The job is almost entirely office-based: a daily round of meetings, writing letters, planning schemes, maintaining links between different sections of the organisation and sorting out problems. The main rewards are the opportunities to set policies and be the single most effective creative force in parks provision in the area.

Training and Qualifications

It is important for managerial staff to have a broad-based horticultural experience, but they must also be academically well-qualified. A degree or HND in horticulture are the most usual qualifications. Students intending to take such courses are encouraged to receive induction training in a parks department by working for a year as a trainee gardener before proceeding to their academic study. Before taking up a managerial appointment, it is also necessary for suitably qualified people to obtain the Institute of Leisure and Amenity Management Diploma. Details from ILAM Education and Training, ILAM House, Lower Basildon, Reading, Berkshire RE8 9NE.

Parks and Playground Attendants

All parks and children's playgrounds within them have attendants who ensure that people using the amenities do so in a proper manner. They are also on hand to help if any accidents happen. As well as this, they have a responsibility to see that their working area is kept tidy and that any play equipment is in a safe condition. No formal training is necessary for these jobs, but most employing authorities like their attendants to have a first-aid certificate, and some will provide training in handling difficult children and their parents.

Working Conditions

Pay is low, and hours are unsocial, involving weekends and, in the summer, evenings. But part-time work is often available, and many people, especially women with families, may find the hours convenient. Being an attendant means you do not have anybody breathing down your neck all the time, and you can, to a certain extent, organise your own working day. However, there may be problems with discipline and vandalism. Groups of youths can run riot in parks and encroach on the playgrounds intended for young children. In these cases you may have to phone the police.

Case Study

Avril and Meg, Playground Attendants

Avril

> When I come in the morning I have to clean the toilets, and then brush the playground, rake the sand, and empty the litter bins. The kiddies come in at lunch time. Sometimes whole classes come with their teachers from nearby schools. I clear up after them and then Meg takes over.

Meg

> Avril and I work in shifts. She does 8 am to 4 pm and I do 4 pm to 9 pm and all day Saturdays and Sundays. During the winter when the playground is shut in the evenings we work together.
>
> I took the job because the money is a bit better than being a barmaid, and the hours fit in with my two children. I don't like working weekends but you have to put up with that when you need the money.
>
> I get the children who come in after school by themselves. I deal with all the minor cuts and bruises (we both did our first-aid certificate) and make sure everyone behaves themselves. And that's not just the children, either! We get people bringing their dogs and letting them foul the place, and I have even seen women push their prams into the paddling pool to wash the wheels. Before I go home, I make sure that everyone has left and that the place is reasonably tidy.
>
> Sometimes vandalism is a problem. There has been thieving from our hut and we get our share of glue sniffers. Most of the time we have a park keeper on duty, or the gardeners are about. But we can be left alone, and then any trouble can be quite frightening.

Wages and Salaries

Manual workers are paid rates similar to those of agricultural workers, and supervisory and management grades have salaries on a par with comparable professionals in local government. With some authorities having to privatise some of their services, particularly gardening and playground supervision it would be sensible for would-be trainees to inquire about the attitude of their local authority in this matter as employment with a private contractor may well be less secure and structured.

Landscaping

Landscaping is the process by which any open space is transformed, given a new look and, sometimes, a new function. Parks, reservoirs, new towns, roadsides and private gardens are among the many areas requiring such consideration, and the process involves two separate activities. The designing and planning is done by a landscape architect and the construction is implemented by landscape contractors. Jobs may take people into either town or country, but are usually organised from an urban base.

Landscape Architecture

Landscape architecture is growing as an organised profession, having currently (1991) just under 3,340 qualified members. It has a rich past on which to draw which survives today in the parks and gardens of stately homes. Its practitioners plan and design all types of outdoor spaces and arrange for their designs to be implemented. It is the task of the landscape architect to reconcile a concern for visual beauty with the demands made upon an area by its function and use by human beings. Jobs may vary enormously, from designing the layout of a small private garden, to preparing landscape plans for large public areas.

As a landscape architect, you will need to have an interest in both art and science, as the process of landscaping is a combination of designers' vision and a knowledge of the practicalities involved in implementing a scheme on a particular site. An awareness of the needs of people, and of their relationship with the environment is essential if your work is to be effective. As one of the interviewees expressed it: 'you need an environmental conscience in the broadest sense'.

Landscape Sciences

Although landscape scientists need to have an understanding of landscape design, their main interest is in the more physical and biological side of landscaping – knowing how to improve waste land and conserve plant and wildlife habitats; forecasting how a new development would affect the local ecology, and developing a programme to minimise its impact. They may have special expertise in botany, ecology or soil science, and will need to study and analyse existing vegetation and wildlife. The work is varied, but many landscape scientists work in research and teaching, or combine research with practice.

Landscape Management
Landscape managers deal with the long-term care and development of new and existing landscapes, and with policy and planning for future landscape management and use. They are involved with amenity and recreation facilities, and with the conservation of scenic and heritage areas. Their work includes the practical management of manpower and machinery, contracting and maintenance budgets.

Training and Qualifications
Associate membership of the Landscape Institute, previously the Institute of Landscape Architects, is the recognised professional qualification.

All applicants must attain graduate membership of the Institute, complete the necessary professional experience and pass the Institute's professional practice examination. The regulations and syllabus for the examination are sent to members when they join the Institute.

As there are at present no specific higher education courses in landscape sciences, and only a few in landscape management, graduate entry qualifications for membership vary between the three disciplines.

For landscape architects, graduate membership of the Institute follows successful completion of graduate and postgraduate courses in their subject. Students are encouraged to become student members of the Institute during their training.

A landscape scientist's first degree should be scientific, such as ecology or natural science. A broad-based course such as environmental studies would need to have a strong scientific content. An appropriate first degree should be followed by a higher degree, such as the MSc in Conservation at University College, London, or MSc in Ecology at Aberdeen, and/or relevant experience. PhD research relevant to landscape work is also acceptable.

The route for a landscape manager would be a degree in natural sciences, plus relevant experience; BSc in Landscape Management at Reading; or an appropriate degree in horticulture followed by a postgraduate course in Landscape Management at Manchester or Wye.

Career Prospects
There is a steady demand for landscape professionals, both at home and overseas, many of whom work as private consultants receiving commissions from public authorities or private clients; others are directly employed by government departments, public bodies, local authorities, industry and new town development corporations.

Salaries are comparable with those of other professions, such as architects, civil engineers and town planners.

Landscape Construction
Most landscape gardeners work for private contractors, as there is a tendency for local authorities and other public bodies to have this work done under contract. Some authorities may, however, employ their own direct labour.

The work of the landscape gardener is to implement the designs for each site. This may involve the levelling and banking of soil, and the construction of walls and pathways as well as planting, fencing and interpreting plans and drawings. The work is, therefore, heavier than most horticultural work, involving basic building techniques and considerable use of machinery.

Training and Qualifications
It is possible to be employed as an unskilled labourer, but the work will be more rewarding if you learn the relevant skills and become a craftsman. Employment and Youth Training provide both on-the-job training and day- or block-release courses at local colleges leading to National Vocational Qualifications recognised by NEBAHAI (National Examinations Board for Agriculture, Horticulture and Allied Industries) or City and Guilds qualifications. Your local Agricultural Training Board office (address in the phone book), Jobcentre or TEC office will give further information on work and training in your area.

Many people wish to be promoted eventually to supervisory or managerial work. To gain the necessary qualifications, you must become a full-time student at an agricultural college. A year's pre-course practical experience on a training scheme may be acceptable for entry to a year's course for the National Certificate in Horticulture (NCH), choosing the amenity horticulture option which often includes some landscaping. Individual colleges may ask for minimum GCSE qualifications and further practical experience. One-year full-time National Certificate courses including Landscape Construction are run at Oaklands College, Hertfordshire; Merrist Wood, Surrey; and Lincolnshire College of Agriculture and Horticulture. Also at Merrist Wood: a three-year sandwich National Diploma course in Horticulture which includes Landscape Construction.

Conditions and Pay
Working as a landscape gardener means moving from site to site with the variety this brings. If you work for a large company, you may sometimes be required to work for short periods away from home, or even to travel overseas.

Rates of pay are similar to those in agriculture (see Chapter 1 pp 22–23) and qualifications are usually acknowledged by an increment scale.

Chapter 4

Forestry

The forestry industry is comparatively small and localised. There are only certain parts of the country, mainly the remote upland areas, where land is used for the growing of trees rather than for agriculture. Forestry is concerned with producing trees, from their planting to the eventual harvesting when they are passed on to the saw mills of the timber trade. About 40,000 people, including office and supervisory staff, are currently employed in forestry and wood processing work, but the industry is expanding as it aims to double timber production by the beginning of the next century.

A Life in Forestry

Forests provide some of the most beautiful landscapes in Britain and, whether you work outside or in an office, they will be part of your working life. For most people who are involved with cultivation, the satisfaction of seeing the plants or crops grow is important. With forestry, there is a long-term return on your work, because even the faster-growing softwoods take 20 to 30 years to reach maturity. But you have the satisfaction of knowing that your work, in whatever capacity, will affect the landscape for a long time to come. It is a job where forward planning is very important because any mistakes you make could last for a long time.

Forestry is very much a job for people who love the countryside, not just when conditions are good, but in all seasons and in all aspects. People working in forestry will find themselves living away from large towns and cities, and must be prepared for the country way of life. For people who work in the woodlands, the job is physically demanding, and can be dangerous. But it is a life spent in beautiful surroundings and close to nature and free of the monotony of many inside jobs.

The Seasonal Round

As with many outdoor jobs, the work is seasonal and this will, to an extent, make for variety in jobs at all levels. Spring is the busiest time when planting takes place, which must be accomplished by the end of April. In summer, the young trees are cared for by clearing the ground around them to allow them room for growth. This may be a monotonous and seemingly endless task, but there is the compensation that it is done during the best weather conditions of the year. In autumn, general maintenance is carried out – thinning out scrubby trees, clearing new areas for planting, and felling the mature trees. Felling, though hard work, can be quite exciting and satisfying, and is a skilled task. Winter is the slackest season when there is time for general work, such as mending fences and gates and clearing rides. Then, in spring, the yearly round begins again.

Recreation

Forests attract many visitors because of their beauty, the wildlife they harbour and the opportunity for field sports. (Pheasants and deer are common inhabitants of woodland areas.) Some landowners employ wardens, rangers or gamekeepers to cater for visitors and their sporting pursuits.

Organisation of the Forestry Industry

The industry is organised in two sectors: public and private. The Forestry Commission is the nationally owned section of the industry, and is responsible for just under half of the total forested area in Britain. The remainder is owned and managed privately in a variety of ways. Conditions of work will vary considerably between the two sectors, the main difference being that the Forestry Commission has a consistent pattern of employment, career structure and pay scales and the private sector does not.

Women and Forestry

The forestry industry is today an almost exclusively male preserve but this need not necessarily continue to be so. During and immediately after the war, a considerable number of women worked in forestry, despite the heavy manual tasks involved at the lower levels of employment. Today, mechanisation has reduced the physical labour so that it is certainly not beyond the reach of many women whose powers of endurance may easily equal those of men. Women are employed in forester and forest officer posts and they are required to gain a year's practical experience of woodland work before embarking on their academic training.

The Forestry Commission

Jobs with the Forestry Commission are secure, and conditions of work and rates of pay are clearly defined. Forest officers are employed for a two-year probationary period, but once this hurdle has been passed it is rare for anyone to lose his or her job.

There are three main levels of employment: forest workers, at the manual or craft grade, forest officers grade IV, whose role is technical, and supervisory and forest officers grade II, who are the managerial staff. As with other forms of outdoor work, moving up the career ladder means moving away from the outdoors to indoor, office-based jobs. However, it is not possible to pass from one level to another by experience alone, as different qualifications are required at each stage.

Forest Workers

As a forest worker you will work with the seasonal round previously described, and be responsible for carrying out all necessary practical work in a woodland area. Apart from the care of trees, planting, pruning, harvesting and nursery work, you will be involved with general maintenance of the forest, such as the clearing of scrub, weeding and drainage and the control of harmful disease or forms of wildlife. You must also be able to turn your hand to fencing and making fire beaters, for example. Forestry is now fairly mechanised and the tools of your trade will be the tractor and the chain-saw which you must be able to use safely.

Each day you will work in the forest and be outdoors except in the very worst of weathers. You will work in a gang headed by a ganger or foreman.

Training and Qualifications

Most forest workers are recruited locally through Forestry Commission district officers. They are untrained but must be physically fit. They learn much of their skill on the job with in-service training courses and block-release college courses. For the first two years new forest workers are sent away on a series of short courses, dealing mainly with the use of mechanical and power equipment, and some may wish to take the City and Guilds (in Scotland, SCOTVEC) exams in forestry. After this trainee period they become qualified forest craftsmen. Craftsmen with suitable experience and personal qualities can be promoted to gangers or foremen.

Working Conditions and Pay for Forest Workers
Some of the equipment can be dangerous so protective clothing must be worn, and this is provided free to all forest workmen. Safety precautions are strictly observed, and no workman is allowed to operate machinery before taking a course of training in its use.

Pay is roughly on a par with that for agricultural workers, and additional experience or training is acknowledged by increments. Basic earnings can be supplemented by production bonuses which can be earned through hard work during the busier seasons.

All forest workers get three weeks' annual holiday as well as all public holidays.

Wardens and Rangers
Wardens and wildlife rangers are usually forest workers who have demonstrated their suitability for this kind of work. Rangers work in the forest, dealing with wildlife control and conservation. They are also responsible for protecting the forest from misuse by visitors. For example, fires are a great hazard in woodland areas and people must be reminded constantly of this. They supervise and maintain facilities for the public, such as car parks and picnic sites, and must be capable of dealing with visitors tactfully but firmly when the need arises. Unfortunately, vacancies are few and much sought after, being filled by forest workers with one or two years' service. Currently the Forestry Commission has developed its visitor services to a maximum so there is no likelihood of further expansion and the creation of new jobs.

Wardens look after the Commission's camp sites and supervise their use during the summer months. Once again, these are popular posts and very few jobs are available.

Pay and conditions for both of these jobs are similar to those for forest workers.

Forest Officers IV

Forest officers grade IV are people with practical forestry experience who have taken further training and are responsible for the annual planning and day-to-day management of a particular forest. In addition, forest officers IV supervise the activities of the workforce and the training of new workers, estimate costs, set piece-work rates and attend to the safety and conservation aspects of the forest. They also liaise with local residents and landowners and, in the first instance, will sort out any problems which arise. They normally work on-site in a small office, but are outdoors for a part of each day dealing with the practicalities of the forestry work.

Training and Qualifications

All forest officers grade IV must hold the BTEC National Diploma, or in Scotland, the SCOTVEC National Certificate with supervising and management levels relevant to forestry; or a degree in Forestry or subject with substantial Forestry content; or corporate membership of the Institute of Chartered Foresters; or City and Guilds Phase IV Certificate in Forestry. A full driving licence is also essential.

The BTEC Diploma in Forestry is available as a three-year sandwich course at the Cumbria College of Agriculture and Forestry, Penrith and Sparsholt College, Hampshire. The Scottish School of Forestry, Inverness, offers a three-year sandwich course leading to a SCOTVEC NC. The colleges take part-time students for in-service training and either the new City and Guilds or SCOTVEC block-release courses at Diploma standard. It is possible for anyone to begin work as a forest worker and later decide to take the ND course. The Forestry Commission does not, however, sponsor employees for this, so study must be undertaken independently, probably with the aid of a local education authority (LEA) grant. If, on the other hand, you are provisionally accepted for the course before you have the necessary work experience, the Forestry Commission will consider you for employment as a forest worker so that you can fulfil this requirement. Further information can be obtained from: The Chief Education and Training Officer, Forestry Commission, 231 Corstorphine Road, Edinburgh EH12 7AT.

Forest Officer II

A Forest Officer II is responsible for the overall planning and administration of forestry in his or her district. This includes private woodlands, as officers act in an advisory capacity to landowners and administer the forestry grants scheme within the area. They may also be involved with the acquisition of land for forestry and in general will fight for good forestry against opposing interests.

There are opportunities for forest officers in all grades to specialise in a particular aspect of forestry and although all jobs are office-based, considerable travelling is involved. This is because close links are maintained with foresters and the work going on in the woodlands.

For administrative purposes, the country is divided into seven conservancies, which are sub-divided into districts. The top posts are in the conservancies where a 'conservator' is assisted by a team of senior managers, each with his or her own speciality (general forest management, harvesting and marketing, engineering, estate work, administration etc). Districts are run by forest District Officers who are employed in junior and senior grades. Most new entrants begin work as a District Officer Grade II, and will have good opportunities for promotion to higher grades after about five years.

Training and Qualifications
All forest officers must have an honours degree in forestry, or an allied subject with a substantial forestry content; or a postgraduate degree in a forestry subject (see Part 2); or equivalent or higher qualification; or corporate membership of the Chartered Foresters. Applicants must hold a full driving licence.

Finding a Job
Recruitment of new entrants at Forest Officer II level is normally through an annual competitive interview arranged by the Civil Service Department, which is usually held in March. Notice of this is given in the national press.

Otherwise, jobs in the supervisory and officer grades are advertised in the following: the Royal Forestry Society's *Quarterly Journal of Forestry* and the national press (particularly the *Daily Telegraph*).

Vacancies for forest workers are often made known by word of mouth, and then verified at the local Forestry Commission Office. So it is a good idea to inquire locally if you are interested. Jobs may also be advertised in the local press.

Case Studies

A Forest Craftsman talks about his work

Martin has lived in the country all his life and works on a small forest near his home.

I've been in forestry for seven years now, ever since I left school. My work hasn't changed at all since I started, but I like it. It's seasonal. In spring we do planting and in summer we cut down the undergrowth from around the young trees. In the autumn we burn up the dead wood and clear the ground for some more tree planting. It's mainly odd jobs in the winter – mending fences, hedging and general maintenance.

When I first started, there were two or three old boys who had been working on the hills for 25 or 30 years, and I picked up the work just by watching them. I was sent to about half a dozen Forestry Commission courses to learn how to use the mechanical equipment (you have to do that for safety reasons) and then, after three years, I was made a forest craftsman. I didn't take the City and Guilds course, but I think you can become a ganger or foreman after you are 30 just with the experience you've got. And I wouldn't want to go higher than that, because then you are in an office most of the time doing paperwork.

Years ago, there used to be 100 men working on the forest. Now there are only five of us. Machinery makes a big difference to the amount of work you can get through, but I think it is also true to say that the forest isn't kept up like it was. A lot of the rides (the grassy paths) are overgrown and fences are in a bad condition. I like working as I do, with just one or two others. It's nice and quiet and you don't get into arguments! We don't work in the rain because we always have the car to sit in and, if bad weather really sets in, we go back to our base and do odd jobs – mending equipment or making fire beaters. There is always plenty to be done. We are on piece work and just get the flat rate if rain sends us in. But in the summer you can earn your money if you are prepared to work.

It *is* hard work and there can be accidents, mainly with the chain-saw, or pulling a muscle in your back lifting the logs. But it's beautiful on the hills, especially in the summer. You see lots of things too, such as birds, deer and foxes. I think it is a job for country people. We had two lads up from the town and they only stuck it for a couple of months. But if you like the countryside and like a nice open-air life, you will like forestry.

A District Forest Officer

David's post is in the West of England, and he has responsibility for many small woodland areas.

I would strongly advise people considering forestry as a career to do a wide degree, such as the Edinburgh course in Land Resources, rather than limiting themselves purely to forestry. This will give them other options should they not find a job. The Forestry Commission is subject to the vagaries of political situations so that one can never tell what will happen.

My job is very varied. I have a basic administrative function and I also deal with the technical side. As far as the work in the forest is concerned, I am responsible for its overall planning, and take decisions about such things as planting and harvesting and fire protection measures. I have close links with the foresters who are more concerned with the practicalities of putting the plans into action.

Another section of my work concerns our relationship with private woodlands. The government grant scheme is operated through the Forestry Commission, and it is my task to administer and advise on grants within my district.

Within the officer grades the further up the ladder you get, the greater the chance of being moved around. I have found this to be the major snag in the job. It has been my personal experience that, as time wears on, these moves become fairly onerous. During my career I have had five major moves, which have taken me all over the country and overseas – although the time abroad was a period of secondment for which I volunteered.

The Private Forestry Industry

Conditions of work are far more haphazard in the private sector than they are in the Forestry Commission, as the industry has so far avoided attempts to impose any standardisation. This means that workers are subject to the attitudes and outlook of their individual employers, and these may vary considerably. The resulting flexibility, however, can be an advantage and may produce a working atmosphere that many people find congenial.

Jobs, as with Forestry Commission work, can be roughly broken down into three groups: forest workers, foresters and managerial staff, but their availability and the qualifications required for them will vary according to the situation and the employer. Manual work will be very similar to that previously described, though the pressure put on employees may be greater because of the profit motive. Graduates are employed for top management positions in large organisations, but otherwise it is quite common for managerial work to be undertaken by the owner of the estate or company. It is often possible to progress to supervisory and even managerial posts on experience alone, but the absence of a clear hierarchy of responsibility at these grades may mean that comparatively fewer opportunities arise. In general, the private sector is characterised by its lack of a clearly defined career structure.

Work situations can be very varied. You might be employed by a large national company with all the anonymity and protection this implies, or you might work for a small private estate, and be subject to an almost feudal situation in which you must show respect and deference to the owner. These are two extremes. In between is a whole range of large and small organisations, each with its own measure of individuality.

Training
If you wish to enter forestry at a managerial level you should first obtain a degree in a forestry subject, and for entry at supervisory grades it is necessary to possess the National Diploma in Forestry (ND), details of which are given on pp 54–55. Jobs as forest workers can be found by both skilled and unskilled people, but if you wish to start in this way and then seek promotion to a higher position, it is sensible to ensure, before you begin work, that you will have the opportunity to take the basic training available for craftsmen. School leavers may be able to enter forestry through Youth Training on the National Preferred Scheme or by contacting their nearest Training and Enterprise Council (TEC). Courses similar to those run by the Forestry Commission are organised for the private sector by the Forestry Training Council (address below). College-based courses at craftsman level are City and Guilds Phases I and II in England and Wales and equivalent SCOTVEC modules in Scotland. As the scheme involves your absence from work on some short courses, you will need your employer's co-operation to take advantage of it. Information about these courses can be obtained from: The Secretary, Timber Growers United Kingdom, Admel House, 24 High Street, Wimbledon, London SW19 5DX; or The Forestry Training Council, Room 413, 231 Corstorphine Road, Edinburgh EH12 7AT.

Employment Opportunities
Employers can roughly be divided into five categories; owners of private estates, national companies, co-operatives, contracting companies, and self-employed sub-contractors.

Private estates. There are a very few large estates which are self-sufficient, even to the extent of having their own saw mills, and these operate entirely with direct labour. On these estates, therefore, there are opportunities for jobs at all levels, except for the top management position which is usually filled by the owner. Smaller estates may employ people in manual and supervisory grades, and many rely on contracting companies for much of the work.

National companies. There are a few large national companies, notably the Economic Forestry Group, Fountain Forestry and Tilhill Forestry, which acquire and manage large blocks of land. They also act on behalf of private owners, providing advice, expertise and labour. These companies employ a large workforce at all levels.

Co-operatives are formed by groups of owners to provide them with management and marketing services. They employ woodland managers and foresters, who either appoint woodmen directly or arrange for work to be carried out by a contracting company.

Contracting companies are independent businesses providing a full range of expertise and manpower for all aspects of woodland management and tree culture. Jobs undertaken may be large or small, commercial or private, adding variety to the day-to-day manual work that it would be hard to find elsewhere.

Self-employed sub-contractors. There has been a tradition in the forestry industry of sub-contract work. Any of the employers mentioned previously may put a job out to sub-contract, and as a sub-contractor you would provide the tools, skills and labour needed. In return, you would be paid an agreed rate for the work. Sub-contractors are involved with manual work and need considerable practical experience and financial backing before setting up alone.

Finding a Job
Most vacancies for woodmen or forest workers are found through word of mouth or are advertised locally, so it is worth asking about openings at local firms. Supervisory and managerial posts are advertised in the journals of the forestry societies and in the national press, and may sometimes be advertised locally.

Case Study
A Forester – a partner in a contracting company

This company, of which my wife and I are partners, is a woodland contracting company – that is, we are prepared to do anything in connection with trees. We supply and plant them, undertake tree surgery and maintenance, and act in a supervisory and consultancy capacity. For this, we employ four managers and up to 26 staff who work in gangs or groups of two and three. We use both direct and sub-contract labour. Sub-contractors are self-employed people who are paid a rate for the job. This has been a tradition in the forestry industry.

We plant 157,000 trees a year in a very short space of time, so the men must be prepared to work in all weathers and must be physically capable of sustained hard work. I would choose someone reasonably intelligent, who has some outdoor background knowledge and whom I could trust. This is important for working in private woodlands. It is still pretty feudal in many of them, and I cannot risk sending a workman who may return home with the odd pheasant or two!

Contracting gives the workforce plenty of interest and constant changes of job and scene. And for someone with an interest in nature it is an opportunity to get to know the countryside well. Even with modern machinery it is still dirty, dangerous and hard work, but it can be fun and rather magnificent.

My responsibility as a forester is great. The decisions I take will have a very long-term effect, because the countryside will bear their mark 100 or 120 years hence. Today, unfortunately, the art of growing trees is subservient to the interests of conservation. Hardwoods – oak, ash, beech and so forth – are thought of as traditional to England, so most grant-aid is structured towards producing them. The trouble is that hardwoods usually require good soil and climatic conditions, which can only be found on agricultural land, whereas softwoods (pines) will grow under the more exacting conditions of the uplands where most forestry is carried out.

As a forester, I see no point in growing a scrubby tree just because it will lose its leaves in winter. It is far better to use poorish land to its best ability, even if this means growing softwoods. We are stewards of our land for the short time we are here and we have a responsibility to improve it, and certainly not leave it any worse. To me, that means planting the best tree that will grow on any given site.

Arboriculture

The Royal Forestry Society defines arboriculture as the establishment, care and maintenance of individual trees for amenity purposes. It gives the chance for those who have not been able to find a place in forestry to work with trees, employed by local authorities, commercial tree surgery firms or botanical gardens. The RFS offers a Certificate in Arboriculture and a Professional Diploma in Arboriculture, both of which can be gained by private study. There are concessionary membership rates for the RFS for full-time students. Details of courses are given on page 105.

Chapter 5

Conservation

Conservationists work with the natural environment from the point of view of its ecology and amenity value. They are concerned with all aspects from purely recreational factors to far-reaching problems in connection with upsetting the natural order by intensive land use or commercial development. People from many disciplines make a contribution to this field; naturalists, planners, landscape architects, ecologists, and those who have gained an intimate knowledge of the countryside through their working experience. Because many of the decisions to be made are complex, and demand a thorough researching of the problems beforehand, this is one of the few work areas described in this book where the proportion of professional (or 'office') staff to manual workers is high. It is also one in which office-based work remains very closely linked with the outdoors, and seldom becomes merely managerial. The quality of the countryside is the reason for the work, and therefore remains the constant source of reference.

The subject is covered in greater detail in *Careers in Environmental Conservation*, published by Kogan Page.

Qualities Required

It is probably true to say that most conservationists are dedicated to the ideals of conservation. In every task there is an issue at stake, and this will filter through, both to those who plan the work and to those who carry it out at ground level. This chapter is concerned mainly with office-based jobs as these are the ones which relate specifically to the subject. Manual work, although directed to the same end, may be very like any other outdoor maintenance work and is therefore described only briefly.

To work in conservation in a planning or managerial capacity you need to have a political sense, as much of the work will involve stating your case and manoeuvring its acceptance past the various committees or authorities involved. You also need an ability to handle people because many of the issues touch on conflicts of interest where persuasion, arbitration and sometimes compromise, must be used. Above all, you must know the countryside well, and the local community whose livelihood is dependent upon it. You must also be able to balance your own ideologies against practical considerations.

Sources and Conditions of Work

As man's ability to tamper with the natural environment increases by leaps and bounds, people have become aware of the urgent need for controls, and conservation is now a growth area of employment. Jobs can be found through both Government and voluntary organisations. The largest employer is local government, followed by central government, mainly through agencies, which are the Countryside Commission and the new Nature Conservancy Councils. Apart from these, there are a number of voluntary organisations, notably local nature conservation trusts, the Royal Society for the Protection of Birds and the National Trust, which offer work. Conditions in the two sectors are rather different in terms of the scope of the work, career structure and remuneration. In general, working for a voluntary body will offer you greater freedom but fewer promotion prospects and a lower salary than employment within Government organisations.

THE GOVERNMENT SECTOR

The Countryside Commission

The Countryside Commission is an official body with an interest in the preservation of the natural environment and its enjoyment by the public. It is mainly an administrative organisation involved with the designation of protected areas (National Parks, Areas of Outstanding Natural Beauty and Heritage Coasts), and is in liaison with both government and local groups involved with the practicalities of conservation, environmental improvement and public access to the countryside. The Commission encourages, and sometimes helps to finance, the setting up of facilities such as car parks, picnic sites, country parks and long-distance footpaths. It also invests in research, by giving grants and financial support to projects provided they seek to further the aims of the Countryside and National Parks Acts.

Grants are available both to organisations and individuals, and the Commission publishes information about their availability. The Countryside Commission, in association with the new Countryside Council for Wales, organises grant-aided and sponsored training courses as part of employers' training programmes through the Countryside Training Unit, Countryside Commission, John Dower House, Crescent Place, Cheltenham, Gloucestershire GL50 3RA. The Countryside Commission also publishes an education and training directory, giving details of full- and part-time courses and other training opportunities for countryside staff.

Nature Conservancy

The former Nature Conservancy Council (GB) was split by the Environmental Protection Act 1990 into three country agencies, taking effect from April 1991.

The three new agencies are: English Nature, responsible for nature conservation in England; the Countryside Council for Wales, a single agency responsible for nature and landscape conservation and also for countryside recreation in Wales; and the Nature Conservancy Council for Scotland, which will merge in April 1992, with the Countryside Commission for Scotland to form Scottish Natural Heritage.

English Nature

English Nature, the Nature Conservancy Council for England, to give it its full title, employs around 150 field, professional and technical grade staff, and around 240 scientific staff, with responsibility for promoting the conservation of wildlife in over 140 National Nature Reserves and around 3,500 SSSIs (Sites of Special Scientific Interest).

The Council acts as an advisory service both to Parliament and to land users, whether they are private landowners, local authorities or members of the public interested in the amenity value of the countryside. Alongside this, it plays an educational role, particularly through the information services on its own reserves. Research is carried out by its own staff, and by people in other organisations who receive grants from the Council.

Working for the Council

Although the Council is not an official Government Department, the conditions it offers employees are similar to those in the Civil Service. Jobs are pensionable, pay scales and holidays are laid down, and there is a defined career structure. For office-based jobs, certain minimum qualifications are required. Posts are geographically widespread through the Council's regional offices but, as the organisation is relatively small and job satisfaction is high, there is strong competition for most vacancies. All posts are open to both men and women, and the Council publishes a booklet, *Employment Information*, obtainable from its headquarters.

Apart from clerical and administrative jobs, there are three main areas of work: scientific, field, and professional and technological.

Scientific Staff

Most scientific staff are employed in the regions where their duties are those of a conservation officer, keeping a watchful eye on all aspects of conservation within their area, and specifically on any Sites of Special Scientific Interest (SSSIs). Scientific staff combine scientific knowledge with public relations work and, at senior levels, are directly involved with the policies of conservation, representing the Council at public inquiries when conservation interests are threatened by development proposals and maintaining contacts with the other country Councils.

There are opportunities for suitably qualified people to work in the Geology and Physiography sections, selecting, assessing and evaluating areas of geological importance and advising on their conservation. These jobs involve liaising with all agencies with an interest in sites, from the government to local landowners.

All scientific officers are graduates, with the exception of some research assistants. Suitable first degree subjects include biology, botany, zoology, geology and physical geography. All previous experience, including any gained in a voluntary capacity, is taken into consideration.

Vacancies are advertised in the *Guardian* and *New Scientist*.

Field Staff

Site managers manage the Council's nature reserves and the job is popular but hard work, demanding a variety of skills and a good deal of physical endurance. Hours may be long, and most of them are spent outdoors in all weathers.

A site manager manages not only the reserve itself, but also the public who visit it. The work includes some general estate maintenance and protection of wildlife, co-ordination of other workers, patrolling and enforcing bylaws, liaising with user groups and some writing of reports.

The Council makes use of voluntary wardens at weekends and holiday times, and working like this is a good way of discovering if the job is for you and is also a recommendation for paid employment; inquiries should be made to your local Regional Office.

Formal educational qualifications are not required, but A levels in biological subjects are a help. Otherwise it is experience and personality which count. You must be a good all-round naturalist and be at least 26, preferably with some prior experience in conservation work. You must also hold a current driving licence and have a good knowledge of vehicle maintenance. You need to be outgoing with people and be able to handle them with firmness and tact. Many people progress to this work after a period as an estate worker.

Jobs are advertised in the national press, *The Field*, *Shooting Times*, *New Scientist* and *Nature* magazines. Successful wardens have the opportunity of promotion to chief warden.

Estate workers carry out the manual labour to preserve the reserves in their original condition and are involved in a variety of outdoor tasks, many requiring forestry skills. The work is hard but it gives a thorough grounding in practical conservation and can lead to other jobs.

Estate workers are recruited locally through the regional offices, to which inquiries can be made. However, jobs are few and far between.

Professional and technological officers

Cartographic draughtsmen are employed to construct and revise maps of National Nature Reserves and Sites of Special Scientific Interest. The minimum qualifications for these jobs are three GCSE passes taken from the following subjects: English, maths, geography, science, a foreign language, art or technical drawing, and surveying.

Land agents are responsible for the acquisition and management of the Council's land and work in co-operation with other staff. Applicants for posts must be corporate members of the Royal Institution of Chartered Surveyors (Land Agency) and should have at least two years' experience. Recruitment is usually at assistant land agent level.

Rates of Pay for Council Staff (1991 Scales)

Scientific Officers
Three grades of employment.   £10,551–£21,797

Site Managers
Three grades of employment.   £10,830–£18,809

Professional and
Technological Officers
Two grades of employment.   £11,146–£22,671

Estate Workers
Basic.   £9,141
Higher grades.   £13,919–£15,546

National Rivers Authority

The National Rivers Authority was set up in 1989 as an independent body to act as a watchdog to protect the water environment. It employs around 6,500 people and operates through 10 regions based on the river catchment areas of England and Wales. Its special responsibilities include the monitoring of water quality, control of pollution, regulation of water supply, flood defences, inland fisheries, conservation and the promotion of recreational facilities such as boating and fishing.

Environmental protection includes the monitoring of sewage effluents, farm pollution and agricultural run-off, landfill waste disposal, and water quality protection. Water quality functions are the responsibility of Water Quality Officers, Pollution Prevention Officers and District Environmental Officers; the scientific section includes chemists, biologists and other scientists.

Fisheries Officers, with water bailiffs and hatchery staff are responsible for maintaining the quality of fishing in rivers and still waters, and for collecting data to indicate river quality.

Conservation includes the protection of SSSIs, wildlife, landscape and historic features. Conservation Officers liaise with the Nature Conservancy councils and local Wildlife Trusts.

Water resources include hydrometric schemes and the collection of data from rain gauges, climate stations, observation boreholes and river flow gauges. Staff include hydrometric technicians, hydrologists and hydrogeologists.

Flood defence is in the charge of a Flood Defence Manager, supported by a Regional Planning Engineer and Regional Operations Engineer. Teams of engineers and technicians monitor data, flood investigations and analysis, and liaise with local bodies on planning applications.

Jobs within the NRA are advertised in the *Guardian, New Scientist* and the local press.

Working for Local Government

Conditions of Work
Conditions of work in local government are well defined. There is a complex career ladder with set salary scales and posts are usually secure. Even in times of financial shortages and cutbacks, it is rare for officers to be made redundant. Most staffing cuts are made by not filling vacant posts. You must be prepared for a slow return on your work, as all recommendations have to go through the bureaucratic machinery before they are agreed, and this is a lengthy process. To some people this is a challenge; to others an annoying impediment.

County Councils
With the increase in nature conservation some city parks departments have conservation officers, but most employment is to be found with rural authorities in the countryside sections of their planning departments. Each authority will employ people with a variety of skills according to local needs, and people with, for example, training in planning, conservation, landscape architecture and forestry backgrounds can usually find work. A degree or professional qualification will generally be a prerequisite.

The main function of a countryside section within the planning department is to monitor proposed development in the area to ensure that it will not be detrimental to issues of environmental concern, so it acts as a controlling and advisory body to those with interests in the land. Most departments also initiate their own projects, either acquiring and managing areas of countryside for conservation or amenity purposes, or liaising with local landowners who are sympathetic to their aims. Tasks are varied and, although mainly office based, will frequently take you out into the countryside.

Case Study

A County Council Planning Officer discusses his work
Ken is the Principal Planning Officer in the countryside section of a very rural authority.

> Our department is fairly typical of countryside sections in county planning. We have a mixture of skilled people: one qualified forester, two landscape architects, one qualified planner and a specialist in recreation planning. We get involved in a whole range of tasks, not least the County Structure Plan, which is a forward planning document which all local authorities have a statutory requirement to produce. Other than this I can give you a list of our involvements: agriculture, forestry, minerals, tourism and the countryside, nature conservation and, to a certain extent, architecture and archaeology. A lot of our time is spent trying to reconcile the conflicting interests of each.
>
> One of the things we have done is to develop demonstration farm projects. We work with a farmer who is willing to try to reconcile all the interests which impinge on his land – but you need to find an enlightened farmer for this! We also work with, for example, the effects of elm losses and the removal of hedges. At the moment we are co-operating with British Waterways to develop a disused canal for its amenity value, and we have a pilot scheme for a peat industry which will be commercially viable without devastating the landscape.
>
> I am a landscape architect. I took the Edinburgh postgraduate course after a geography degree. I started work in the late 1960s when the new towns were at their zenith, and that is where I found my first job. It was a good way of getting first-hand experience of doing work on the ground. The speed of development was such that you could design a scheme and then see it being done the next day.
>
> After that, I had the choice between private practice and local government and I opted for the latter. My choice was based on a belief that I could use my skills to best effect within the statutory framework. This country is still a long way behind the USA in its concern for the environment, and there is a great need for watchdogs and well-balanced advice on environmental issues. Most issues have to do with a style of environmental education which is linked to ecology. You must try to produce patterns of life which relate to the environment. Sadly, though, many planners disregard these matters. They need to be controlled, and to have someone who will prod their environmental conscience. And I think if you work for local government, you carry more weight when you attempt this role.
>
> On average, I spend two days a week out of the office, but I would like it to be more. Most of the time is spent talking to farmers and

landowners, cajoling and persuading – which are necessary activities if I am to get them round to my way of thinking. The more time I spend in this way, the more productive I consider it to be. The land is our basic resource in the work we do and if we don't spend enough time on it we are failing in our duty.

Working in a National Park

There are 11 national parks in England and Wales of which 8 are run as departments of local government. They were designated in the 1950s as being of national interest because of the beauty of their countryside. This does not mean, however, that they are publicly owned. The areas they cover are large (the one I visited stretches for 169,600 acres and is one of the smallest) and most of the land is in private hands. Nevertheless, the staff who work in a national park have responsibility for the whole area and legislation recently proposed should increase their control over private development within the boundaries. Their two main functions are to preserve and enhance the natural beauty and to promote the enjoyment of the countryside by the public. Where any conflict arises between these two functions, preservation is paramount. In the future, a third objective may be added to this list: to have regard for the economic and social well-being of the local community, but this has not yet become a statutory obligation.

As with most jobs in conservation, you will be working not only with the natural environment, but with people as well. In the national parks there is what may be termed an 'eternal triangle' of countryside, community and visitors and it can be difficult to reconcile the interests of all three. Intensive tourism can damage the countryside; farmers and visitors can come into conflict over such matters as rights of way and trespass; and the need for farmers to make a living can cause them to inflict lasting change on the character of the land. Public relations will therefore play a large part in the work.

The Structure of a National Park Team

Each park will differ, according to the individual characteristics of the countryside, in the specialist help employed, but, in general, jobs may be divided into three categories: officers, wardens or rangers, and estate workers.

Officers have an allotted role and are in constant contact with the countryside in very much the same way as their counterparts in county planning. Positions will include those with responsibility for development and forward planning, for educational and visitor services, and for estate management. There will also be a number of specialist posts in areas relevant to the needs of the particular park, for instance in agriculture, ecology or forestry.

A first requirement is an ability to work with people persuasively and with tact. Apart from this, you should have an intimate knowledge of the local countryside and its inhabitants, and a degree or professional qualification to equip you for any specialist work you undertake. Most national parks are situated at a distance from large towns or centres of population, so you must be prepared for a rural way of life.

Wardens and Rangers are the link between the officers and the visitors. They are responsible for monitoring the state of the countryside and its visitor services, such as footpaths, viewpoints and car parks. During the tourist season, they travel the area meeting the public, offering help and advice and also ensuring that amenities are properly used. They are also usually the people best known to local farmers and landowners, and may find themselves the first port of call when disputes or problems arise.

The job of a warden or ranger is a solitary one, so you must like working alone and on your own initiative. You must be able to sustain first-hand contact with residents and visitors, and have an understanding of their needs as well as those of the countryside. It is difficult to confine this kind of work within set hours, so you need to be prepared for irregularity and be tolerant of disturbed evenings and weekends.

There are no formal qualifications which will ensure you a job. Posts are much sought after, and several hundred people may apply for each vacancy. Above all, what is needed is an appropriate life experience, and it is rare for a young person, however well qualified, to be appointed to a post.

Estate Workers. In all national parks some proportion of the land is government owned, and this must be maintained in much the same way as any other estate. Car parks must be constructed, fencing kept in order, footpaths signposted and cleared and areas of forest maintained. The work is varied, and will take you to a different part of the countryside each day. It will also be free of the cap-touching feudal undertones which still exist on many private estates.

Case Studies

A National Park Warden talks about his life
Jim is the Head Warden, with a staff of three, and has been in his post for 20 years.

I love this countryside and my job. I came from a farming family and ran away to sea when I was 14, but I always returned here for my holidays.

When I came here, there was nobody else. The office staff were not appointed until the reorganisation of local government in 1974, and my only boss was miles away in County Hall. My brief was to pick up a Land-rover and help the public enjoy the amenities of the national park. It was a marvellous opportunity to make the job what I wanted it to be. Over the years I have got the good will of the farmers and landowners – without which you can't do the job. You must create a happy atmosphere between them and the visitors.

I started on 1 June, and I was in at the deep end immediately, because the tourist season was just beginning. My first move was to drive around in the Land-rover making myself known to any visitors I met, and just hope they wouldn't ask any awkward questions! Mostly they asked me the way to places, or complained that they had tried using footpaths marked on the map but had lost their way. There was no signposting of footpaths in those days, and many were overgrown. So I decided that my first task was to tackle this problem and I started the Waymark Walk Scheme which has since won a national award. It's so simple: a matter of erecting signposts with the distance and destination, plus a coloured square. This colour is then repeated at intervals along the route.

The biggest part of the job is public relations, and the Walkway Scheme helped with this. It meant that visitors were no longer straying from the path and trespassing, or disturbing residents during their leisure hours to ask the way. When they saw the way things were going, landowners began to co-operate and asked me to mark the paths running across their land. For the first 12 years, I spent every winter just working on opening up the paths linking villages together. In the summer I am always busy with visitors, driving between the various car parks and viewpoints, meeting them and talking to them, giving them help and information and making sure they use the amenities properly. I work with school parties too, leading adventure walks and talking to them.

There are three other wardens, apart from myself, and we are organised to work in areas. I insist that we take no leave during June, July and August which are our busiest months. It's no job for a 9 to 5 person.

What we need for this job is an idea of the way of life on these hills, of the people who live here and the way they work. For a warden in another area it might be different. In a green belt area, for example, it might be more important to be a naturalist; in the Lake District you might need someone with a knowledge of climbing. You can't generalise. Warden posts are very hard to get, and anyone with any sense would stay put, as I have done, once they have one.

Tony, an Estate Manager, describes his work for a National Park

I am responsible for the direct management of 6,000 acres, which is the area owned by the national park. I am in charge of the day-to-day work of the estate force which carries out all necessary maintenance, and I liaise on a daily basis with the foreman. I allocate priorities to jobs.

Apart from running the estate, I provide a link between the wardens and the headquarters – that is, I deal with the amenity aspect of the national park. I manage such things as the legal aspects of rights of way, and I sometimes get involved with management agreements with landowners. Usually I try to achieve as much for everybody as possible. I also take decisions which will affect tourists. Excessive recreation can very often spoil the magic of the place they have come to see, so numbers of visitors have to be watched very hard and controls set up where necessary.

My work is mainly managerial, and differs very little from that of any estate manager. I process works contracts, make reports, attend meetings and liaise with other interested bodies. I also have a knowledge of machinery. That's important in times of money shortage. We cannot afford to buy the wrong machine for the job.

I have a practical attitude to my work. For 20 years I was in the Household Cavalry, but have always been very much attached to this part of the world. I know the country well, and I know the people who work in it. I know about their farming practices and I accept the rural way of life: the shoots, the hunts and the fishing. I think this is very important. You can't take the right decisions without having an intimate knowledge of the bit of countryside for which you are responsible. You have to know the facts of life. If a herd of moorland ponies grows too large, there is only one thing to be done, and if someone fells a tree with a chainsaw, there's no point in screaming. (The tree was probably near the end of its life, anyway.) Farmers have to be down-to-earth in order to survive, and I respect this.

WORKING IN THE VOLUNTARY SECTOR

Working for a voluntary organisation has its rewards and its drawbacks. The rewards are in terms of the freedom usually given to staff to develop their own style of work and operate independently at the decision-making level; the drawbacks relate to salaries (which are usually low) and the small size of most working units (which do not offer much of a career ladder).

Money is tight and most organisations prefer to spend it on employing staff at officer level, relying on voluntary help for general maintenance. This means that opportunities for people without higher educational qualifications are limited, and those who do find work must be prepared to co-operate with volunteers. Work in the voluntary sector is not for the union man or woman, who will demand conditions the employer is unable to provide.

The RSNC Wildlife Trusts Partership

This is the largest voluntary organisation formerly known as the Royal Society for Nature Conservation, concerned purely with conservation and is a partnership representing the interests of 46 Wildlife Trusts and 50 Urban Wildlife Trusts spread throughout the UK. Each Trust is a member of the partnership and, although affiliated to the central society, is an independent voluntary body whose activities depend upon available funding and other local conditions. Currently, there are 500 salaried staff; each Trust has between 4 and 30 officers.

Job vacancies can vary according to whether or not grants are increased to the individual Trusts; though some Trusts now have stable funding. There are opportunities for people with degrees in subjects such as biological sciences, ecology and conservation, or for those who have gained considerable experience through working with the natural environment. There is also a need for PR and marketing skills.

Working Conditions
Salaries are likely to remain lower than those in the public sector. In the past, Trust work was seen as a stepping stone to a more substantial position in state-sponsored nature conservancy or local government, but the Trust movement is now beginning to develop its own career structure. Some Wildlife Trusts are becoming more established and it is possible to think of a career in terms of graduating from a small Trust to a large one.

The Work of the Trusts
The scope of the work will depend on the size of the Trust and local pressures on wildlife. Large ones are involved in a variety of tasks. They may acquire and manage areas of land as nature reserves; they will run educational programmes and form links with local schools and colleges; and they will keep a watch on proposed land

development in the country. When necessary, they will intervene and try to influence the form such development takes, or even try to stop it altogether. Where funding is available, Trusts will sponsor research projects based on the local environment, designed either to fill gaps in knowledge, or to support proposals they are making with regard to land use and development. They will be generally available in an advisory capacity and will liaise with land users and other interested bodies. In smaller Trusts, officers are involved in a wider variety of work.

Employment Opportunities
Employment is usually available in three ways: (1) permanently, (2) on a contractual basis for the length of a project, and (3) seasonally.

Conservation Officers are the key workers in any Wildlife Trust, and are usually permanent employees. Their role is to initiate and co-ordinate the work of the Trust and the work they do falls into two categories. First, they need to know about land management and to arrange for necessary maintenance to be carried out by volunteers. They may also be required to act as advisers on land management, both to their own members (most Trusts obtain a proportion of their funding from membership subscriptions) and to outsiders such as water and forestry authorities. Second, they are involved in the assessment of the value of conservation sites, whether these are owned by the Trust or not. They also run the campaigning side of the Trust's activities, and monitor the likely implications of land development.

Most conservation officers are graduates with some post-graduate training or work experience in nature conservancy or local government.

Project Officers are usually employed on a three-year contract, funded by grant aid to conduct a specific survey or develop a particular project. They must have experience in research methods, a relevant educational background and familiarity with a specific subject – such as otters and rivers, for the work they will be doing.

Reserve Wardens. On nature reserves, wardens are sometimes employed to provide facilities for the public such as signposting and labelling, to carry out general maintenance and to manage and assist visitors. This is a job for the naturalist with a practical bent, and though graduates may take on the work, people whose experience comes from working on the land and with wildlife may be just as suitable. At present there are not many permanent posts available, and most are on a seasonal basis, but with the continued development of the Trust movement, more permanent posts may emerge. A good first step would be to join your local Wildlife Trust; jobs, paid or voluntary, are advertised in the newsletter.

Case Study

A Conservation Officer considers his role
Rob works for a small Trust, which also employs an education officer and, currently, two project officers.

I went to Cambridge to read geography, but switched to applied geography in my last year. This gave my work the slant I wanted, and I then went on to take the MSc in Conservation at University College in London. It happens to be the only postgraduate course purely on conservation in the country.

My first job was with the Nature Conservancy Council doing a vegetation survey in Northumbria, and then I had a spell in local government.

Having had the experience of working for the statutory authorities, I intend to stay in the voluntary sector. There is nothing I'd rather do. I have the freedom to assess what is important to deal with and to direct resources as I think fit. Much of the work involves setting up projects and employing teams of graduates to carry them out. So I'm now very much in the business of organising other people. That is how the job develops, once you are established.

I now think of myself as an active conservationist in the political sense, rather than as a naturalist. There are other people who have more specialist knowledge than me, and I would go to them for information. Many of them may be volunteer workers, and I think it is necessary to stress the importance of being able to work with volunteers. They are not a captive workforce, so there are no 'defined relationships' and often they may know more about certain things than you. They also bring their own quite strong specific interests, and sometimes these have to be balanced, one against the other. This is my task, and tact and persuasion are needed!

The National Trust

The National Trust is the largest single charitable organisation devoted to conservation in the British Isles. The main emphasis of the Trust's activities is on preservation, and to this end it owns or manages areas of country and coastline as well as historic houses and gardens. The National Trust operates in England, Wales and

Northern Ireland, and there is a separate organisation in Scotland, the National Trust for Scotland, which has its headquarters in Edinburgh.

The Trusts receive many inquiries from people wishing to work for them and emphasise that, as they usually do not keep waiting lists of would-be employees, there is little point in writing to them except in reply to a particular job advertisement. They do, however, produce leaflets outlining opportunities for employment, which are obtainable from their head offices (see p 110). As the total workforce is relatively small, vacancies do not occur very frequently.

Land Agents are employed in the regional offices to deal with the day-to-day management of the houses and estates. As well as the normal duties of estate management, they are involved with the more specialised problems of the care of historic buildings and their contents, nature conservation, and relations with the visiting public.

To become a land agent you must have passed the examination of the Royal Institution of Chartered Surveyors in the Land Agency and Agricultural Division, and have at least two or three years' professional experience.

Vacancies are advertised in the *Chartered Surveyor*.

Gardeners are employed on most National Trust properties on scales ranging from unskilled assistant to head gardener of a large garden. People working at the highest level will not only be skilled horticulturalists but will also have responsibility for the overall management of the garden and the gardeners who work there.

Young people are encouraged to attend day-release classes to obtain a recognised qualification. The Trust provides Youth Training for around 36 school leavers a year who want to specialise in amenity horticulture, forestry or countryside management. Practical experience is supplemented by two-weeks' residential college training, and trainees are encouraged to go on to further education. Head gardeners usually have a National Diploma (ND); Botanic Garden Diploma; College Certificate; or the equivalent in horticulture.

Vacancies are advertised in the local press and in *Horticulture Week*.

Forestry Staff. Much of the Trust's estate land is woodland, and there are openings for people to work on the maintenance of these areas. There are two main grades of employee: assistant foresters, who are responsible for the day-to-day work, and foresters who work in a supervisory capacity. The work is similar to other forms of forestry without the commercial interest.

Foresters are recruited untrained, and training is given in special skills. Head Foresters normally have BTEC NC, OND or City and Guilds Phase II. Senior members of staff have a degree or ND in Forestry.

Vacancies are advertised in the local press and in the journal of the Royal Forestry Society.

Wardens are employed in much the same capacity as parks attendants. They are responsible both for simple maintenance (such as the repair of signs and fencing) and for supervision of visitors. For this job, you must be able to deal firmly and tactfully with people, and to give information when required. No special qualifications are necessary, but the work is demanding and entails long hours spent out of doors, often on weekends and bank holidays.

Advisory Staff. A small team of highly specialised staff works from the Cirencester office to advise on the management and conservation aspects of the Trust's estates. Higher academic qualifications in subjects such as conservation, ecology, forestry or horticulture are required for these posts.

The Royal Society for the Protection of Birds (RSPB)

The RSPB is a well-established society concerned with the protection of birds and their habitats throughout the British Isles. Its network of activities is extensive, and it is able to offer rather better conditions of employment, in terms of career structure and salaries, than many of the smaller voluntary organisations.

Most jobs with an outdoor bias are in the conservation division of the Society, and are concerned with the running of around 118 nature reserves, the protection of rare breeding birds, advisory work and research, and monitoring and taking political action on development proposals and land use practices which may pose a threat to birds and their habitats. Within this division, people are employed to fulfil three main functions: management, research, and the provision of a warden service.

General Qualities Required

The RSPB provides the opportunity for some people to turn a hobby into a career. To work in any capacity in the organisation, you must be a keen ornithologist and have a wide knowledge of birds. As with all jobs in conservation, public relations work is important as you will often be faced with the task of balancing opposing interests. Management skills will be required for the higher positions and, if you wish to work in the research team, you must have appropriate scientific education at degree level.

The Warden Service

The Warden Service is the field in which most people begin their work for the RSPB, either as a seasonal employee or a volunteer. It is organised in two sections: the Reserves and the Species Protection Departments.

Reserve Wardens. There are a few vacancies for permanent wardens on the Society's reserves, but these are very sought after. It is usual to begin as a volunteer warden during the summer months, and then proceed to paid seasonal work. Temporary summer wardens are employed from the beginning of April to the end of August, and people taking these jobs usually return for several years while awaiting a permanent vacancy.

Permanent wardens are employed on a particular reserve, graduating from assistant to head warden. In the senior grade, you will have the responsibility for the management of the reserve and for organising voluntary help. Wardens undertake the task of attracting birds to the reserve and of providing the right breeding conditions, carrying out bird counts and producing an annual report. There is a lot of contact with the visiting public, both through providing information and through supervising their use of the reserve.

Species Protection Wardens are employed only on a seasonal basis from April until August, and either stay in one location to protect nesting sites or are mobile throughout a defined area. In the latter case, their task is to monitor the bird population and undertake work with the public to ensure that rare birds are not put at risk. At the end of the season, species protection wardens may be required to submit a report on their activities. Most jobs are in lonely parts of the country – predominantly in the Highlands, the Lake District and Central Wales.

Qualifications Required

No formal educational qualifications are needed to become a warden, but you must have a good knowledge of birds and be a keen naturalist. Many wardens have a degree, but this is not a necessary requirement as long as you have a good level of general education and can tackle writing reports. If you work alone as a species protection warden, you must have initiative and the ability to live rough while you are on the move – and also to work all hours. You need to be outgoing (though able to live a solitary life) because a large part of your work will concern relations with the public, both local residents and visitors. Normally, you will need to be over 20 before being considered for employment.

Working Conditions and Pay

All wardens are provided with free accommodation according to local conditions. This may be in a cottage, or converted outbuildings or, in more outlying areas, in a caravan. Travelling expenses for on-the-job journeys are paid.

Finding a Job

Vacancies are often heard about on the grapevine in ornithological circles. They are also advertised in the RSPB's magazine *Birds*, and sometimes in other journals such as *British Birds* and *BTO News*, the news-sheet of the British Trust for Ornithology.

Salaries in Conservation – a General Picture

Salaries within the voluntary sector of conservation work vary greatly according to local conditions and may sometimes be very low. However, all officers working for local government or other government agencies will be paid according to a well-defined system, usually on a par with comparable professionals such as planners, architects and research officers.

Chapter 6
Rural Crafts

In recent years there has been an increased respect for and interest in the work of the craftsman. With easy transport of materials, many crafts such as weaving, pottery and furniture-making are no longer essentially rural and can just as well be carried on in a city, but there are still a few traditional skills which have their roots in the countryside and a rural way of life.

Craft work will appeal to people who are creative and have a respect for tradition and natural materials. To take up a craft, you must have patience, a feeling for the materials with which you work and you must like using your hands rather than being involved with mechanical processes.

It would be uncharacteristic for such activities to be conducted under the auspices of big business. If you work in a rural craft, you will be involved in a small family concern, or even set up under your own initiative. Some crafts have their own professional organisations; others do not. The main thread which draws them all together is the Rural Development Commission which offers a service in three ways. It has offices in most county towns from which field officers work, providing the first point of contact; it also runs an advisory service with expertise in all aspects of small rural industries and it operates a loan scheme to help people start up. It has a concern for training, and runs short courses in aspects of small business management and grant-aided two-year schemes for young employees or rural enterprises. Crafts currently offered include the following: thatching, leatherwork, wrought-iron work, furniture restoration, upholstery, farriery, woodwork and pottery. Inquiries can be made to the head office at 141 Castle Street, Salisbury, Wiltshire SP1 3TP, or to local offices whose telephone numbers will be found in the directories of the county towns concerned.

The following examples are only three of the activities which may be listed under the headings of rural crafts. It is by no means to be considered as an exhaustive list of the kinds of work available.

Willow Growing and Basket Making

Basket making from willow or osier is one of the oldest crafts, but today is carried out by fewer than 100 professional workers. Some are employed in small industries, some as home workers, and others are self-employed, either selling their wares in their own shops or supplying other retailers.

There is no organisation for training, and one learns on the job, but most skilled basket makers are only too willing to pass on their knowledge to young entrants to the craft. Most basket makers are men, as the work is hard on the hands and demands considerable strength, especially for larger items.

Willow growing is mainly confined to the Sedgemoor area of Somerset, as the drainage of land elsewhere for agricultural use (notably in Norfolk) has driven the willow crop out. The work is part agricultural and part craft, and is very labour-intensive as the industry is too small to be mechanised.

Willows are propagated in March from cuttings, and harvested each winter from the third year until the end of their lives, 20 or 30 years later. They need constant attention and protection from aphids which render them useless for basketwork. The harvested rods are sorted for size and prepared for use through a number of skilled processes.

Case Study

Chris and Anne, Willow Growers and Basket Makers

Most basket makers don't grow their own willow. We are unusual in combining the two processes. It is traditional in our family. The industry has been carried on here for 150 years. It is a skill which is handed down from generation to generation – you can't go to college to learn how to grow willow.

We have always had our willow beds, but there was a slump in the demand for craftwork for a time and we stopped that side of things, replacing it with general agricultural work. When demand increased, we started basket making again, and this is what we want to do as we feel very strongly that it is a craft which should not be allowed to die. It was difficult at first because most of the skilled people were nearing retiring age, but we now have a team of five young workers trained by the older men who have now given up. We are planning to introduce basket furniture making soon, and are getting the only skilled man in this area, now in his 80s, to come and instruct our team. That's the way it is. You have to catch on to the old expertise before it is gone forever.

There is no telling who will make a good basket maker. You need someone who is practical, has a love of natural materials and is also creative. A lot of the work is instinctive – having an eye for shape and balance and being able to handle the willow. We have our failures and sometimes we have to advise people, for their own sake, as well as ours, that the craft is not for them. But most of our workers stay – to their satisfaction as well as ours.

On the cultivation side we also have five workers. We grow 30 acres of willow, and there is enough to keep them busy all the year. We don't employ casual labour. Times of the year not occupied by actual cultivation are given over to processing the harvested crop. This is a craft job. Once the rods have been sorted for size, they are boiled so that the bark will strip. This also gives them the traditional warm brown colour. The stripped rods are then propped up outside to dry, and finally they are bundled, ready for use. By changing the process we can get white or dark brown rods, but we use no dyes. We use about a third of our crop ourselves; the rest we sell.

We pay our workers agricultural wages and try to pay our craftsman basket makers slightly more. But it is a chancy business. Recently, our crop failed for two successive years and that hit us hard. We need something to fall back on, so we now produce artists' charcoal which we supply to the main national firms. It is made from willow fired in a special kiln to a high temperature. The demand for this is constant, so it is economically essential to us.

We are pleased that we have now centred all our activities on the willow. It is traditional to this area and we are making our contribution to keeping this tradition alive.

Thatching

Thatching is also an ancient craft, and very much alive today. The skill is passed on from master to apprentice, but there is also a training scheme organised by the Rural Development Commission which takes 16 apprentices each year. The course lasts for two years. The apprentice works with a master thatcher and attends a number of week-long residential courses at Wellingborough during the training period. On-the-job training is constant, and the master receives a grant for his help in the process.

Case Studies

A Master Thatcher and his Apprentice
Bob has run his own small business for 12 years. When I spoke to him, he and his apprentice, Simon, were on their first day of re-thatching a country cottage.

Bob

A medium-sized cottage like this will take two of us between four and six weeks to thatch. You can do it alone, but it means more running about, up and down the ladder, collecting the reeds. We are using local wheat reed for this. It has to be laid wet so we soak it the night before. We also use water reed – it used to be called Norfolk reed – which has to be laid dry. But that we can't get locally; it has to come from Scotland, or even Holland.

Before I left school, like everybody else I wanted something to do in the holidays. I knew a thatcher, so I worked for him and later he gave me the opportunity to carry on with him. I took my apprenticeship for five years, finishing when I was 19, and then my boss died so I either had to carry on by myself or do something else. If the work is there, you can set up by yourself very cheaply. All you need is a ladder, the reed, your tools, most of which you can make yourself, and a vehicle to carry them all in. I had the advantage of being known through working with my late boss, so I decided to go it alone and I've never looked back. I never have to go far away. There is always plenty of work in these parts. I have been lucky not to run into non-payers. A couple of customers who don't pay up can ruin a young person starting as I did, alone and with no backing.

I worked by myself for the first three or four years, then I took on apprentices. Simon has been with me for six months now, and he will do a four-year training. The main trouble for young people wanting to take up the craft is that there are too few openings. An apprentice cannot lay on reed immediately. It is not like a labouring job – it has to be learned. This means that you can only really do with one apprentice at a time as it is a one-to-one training. There are other problems too. During the training period the pay is bad, although the prospects afterwards are good, and it's not the best of jobs for winter. I am a country man myself, but I admit it can be tough in bad weather. You get a lot of townies thinking they'll like it, but they don't survive the first winter!

The only thing that stops us working is rain, and when that happens we use the time to make spars out of hazel or withy. They are the pins which hold the thatch in position. A few years back, when we had those heatwaves, we had to start work at 4.30 or 5.00 in the morning. By midday it was too hot to be out on a roof with the vapour rising from the damp reeds.

One of the interesting things I've done is to work for the BBC and Pinewood Studios, doing thatching on a film set. I was at Pinewood for about seven weeks – a bit of a change from the quiet life around here!

Simon

I just heard about thatching through my uncle who knows Bob. It sounded interesting and I thought I would give it a try. I began when

I was 16 after I left school, and so far I have enjoyed it. When I started I just carried the reeds for Bob and swept up. Now I do the tying in and we both work on the roof together. I think it will be interesting to do the thatching course, and I certainly intend to finish my apprenticeship. I know I haven't been through the winter yet, but I expect I'll manage it!

Gamekeeping

Gamekeeping is a craft involving the raising of game birds for sport and their management during a shoot. Traditionally, gamekeepers worked on private estates and were involved with the complete control of wildlife within their territory. Now, however, there is an increasing tendency for shoots to be organised co-operatively, and even commercially, by large syndicates. This has changed the methods used as large numbers of birds are required to cater for the demand.

Case Study

A Gamekeeper talks about his work
Bill is an experienced gamekeeper and now, in a contracting market, considers himself fortunate to be working on a private estate.

I've been a gamekeeper all my life like my father and grandfather before me. In the old days it used to be passed down from father to son. I worked for 22 years on the same estate, and then got a job with a commercial syndicate. I didn't like the way things were there, or see eye to eye with my boss, so left to come here.

My job is to rear the pheasants and keep the estate free of vermin so that they survive. I take the work in seasons, preparing the laying pens and sitting boxes, ready for when the hens start laying at the beginning of April. Then I have to look after the eggs and turn them every day to stop the yolks setting, and when I have enough they are put with the broody hens in the sitting boxes. The chicks hatch in late May or early June, and stay in a rearing hut at first. Then I gradually get them used to the open by putting them in a pen or field with the broody hens. That is when your worry starts, because you have to keep the hawks and magpies off. When the chicks are six weeks old you take them to cover (that is, release them in a wood) and they stay there for a lifetime. You feed them twice a day until the end of the season.

This is the traditional method. These days, many people buy their eggs or rely on wild stock if they only have a small shoot for their own sport, and this cuts out a lot of the work.

The season starts at the beginning of October and continues until the end of January. You get attached to the pheasants. Part of the skill of a gamekeeper is to get the birds in the right place so that they will rise over the guns when they are disturbed by the beaters. You have to be prepared for this. After a shoot, I go over the estate to find any injured birds. I don't leave them to suffer. The lucky ones survive – a lot of them do, really.

To be a gamekeeper you have to know the land like the back of your hand; to know where the foxes go and where the badger runs are. You also need to know what crops are near at hand, because pheasants are roaming birds and it can be a headache stopping them going for attractive food. They like corn and root crops mainly. Once they are on someone else's land you have no control over them, so you have to get them back.

I patrol around the estate pretty often, so I don't have much trouble with poachers. If I find them I fire over their heads. In the old days you used to get gypsies taking Christmas trees and holly to sell at Christmas but that is not so much of a problem today. You have to know the people on the estate, and the neighbours too, and work with them; otherwise the job is very difficult. And you never see a good gamekeeper without his dog. You need a reliable dog with you always, especially for retrieving and ferreting.

It is a dying profession now. Estates are splitting up and many private owners cannot afford to maintain their own sport. Some form cooperatives with other neighbouring owners to share costs, but in the main it is the commercial syndicates that have taken over. There are foreigners who will pay a lot of money to shoot many birds, and for this you have to keep the birds flying over all the time. The syndicate I worked for briefly had five keepers raising 26,000 chicks a year. That's not what I call sport. It's more or less slaughter.

There are a few openings for young people as trainees, but generally the job is not what it was.

Part 2

Chapter 7

Courses and Qualifications

Most full-time courses in agriculture, horticulture and forestry require students to have at least one year's practical experience at the outset. Useful contacts for arranging this experience are listed in Chapter 8. Apart from academically based courses, there are wide opportunities for in-service training at craftsman level. For a career in conservation the picture is not so clear, but some of the more usual routes are discussed below.

Degree Courses

Students applying for degree courses must have the usual academic requirements for entry to a university; that is, at least five GCE/GCSE passes (in Scotland SCEs), of which two must be GCE A levels. As the courses are science-based, intending students should be suitably qualified in science subjects.

All applications are made through the Universities Central Council on Admissions (UCCA). Five choices may be entered on the UCCA form. As courses vary considerably, it is sensible to obtain a prospectus for each before making a choice.

Applications should be made between 1 September and 15 December of the year preceding the intended start of studies. Candidates applying to Oxford must submit a preliminary application form, *in addition to the UCCA form*, by 30 September to the address given in the course list below.

Applications for polytechnic degree courses should be made through the Polytechnic and Colleges Admissions Service (PCAS), but applicants should check with the college.

Courses in Agriculture

Aberdeen
The University of Aberdeen, 581 King Street, Aberdeen AB9 1UD

Aberystwyth
University College of Wales, Department of Agricultural Sciences, Penglais, Aberystwyth, Dyfed SY23 3DD
University of Wales, Welsh Agricultural College, Llanbadam Fawr, Aberystwyth, Dyfed SY23 3AL
Ashford
Wye College, Wye, Ashford, Kent TN25 5AH
Bangor
University College of North Wales, School of Agriculture, Bangor, Gwynedd LL57 2DG
Belfast
The Queen's University, Faculty of Agriculture and Food Science, New Forge Lane, Belfast BT9 5PX
Chelmsford
Writtle College, Chelmsford, Essex CM1 3RR
Cirencester
Royal Agricultural College, Cirencester, Glos GL7 6JS
Edinburgh
Faculty of Science Office, West Mains Road, Edinburgh EH9 3JG
Newcastle
University of Newcastle upon Tyne, Newcastle upon Tyne NE1 7RU
Newport
Harper Adams Agricultural College, Newport, Shropshire TF10 8NB
Newton Abbot
Seale-Hayne College, Newton Abbot, Devon TQ12 6NQ
Nottingham
University of Nottingham, School of Agriculture, Sutton Bonington, Loughborough, Leicestershire LE12 5RD
Reading
University of Reading, Faculty of Agriculture and Food, Whiteknights, PO Box 217, Reading RG6 2BU

Postgraduate Courses
Bedford
Silsoe College, Cranfield Institute of Technology, Silsoe Campus, Bedford MK45 4DT
Biggleswade
Shuttleworth College, Cranfield Institute of Technology, Old Warden Park, Bedfordshire SG18 9DX
Chelmsford
Writtle College, Chelmsford, Essex CM1 3RR
Newport
Harper Adams Agricultural College, Newport, Shropshire TF10 8NB

Nottingham
University of Nottingham School of Agriculture, Sutton Bonington, Loughborough, Leicestershire LE12 5RD
Reading
University of Reading, Department of Agriculture, Earley Gate, PO Box 236, Reading RG6 2AT

Courses in Horticulture

Ashford
Wye College, Wye, Ashford, Kent TN25 5AH
Bath
The University, Claverton Down, Bath BA2 7AY
Chelmsford
Writtle College, Chelmsford, Essex CM1 3RR
Cirencester
Royal Agricultural College, Cirencester, Glos GL7 6JS
Nottingham
University of Nottingham, School of Agriculture, Sutton Bonington, Loughborough, Leicestershire LE12 5RD
Reading
University of Reading, Faculty of Agriculture and Food, Whiteknights, PO Box 217, Reading RG6 2BU
Strathclyde
The University of Strathclyde, Glasgow G1 1XW

Postgraduate Courses
Nottingham
University of Nottingham, School of Agriculture, Sutton Bonington, Loughborough, Leicestershire LE12 5RD
Reading
University of Reading, Department of Agriculture, Earley Gate, PO Box 236, Reading RG6 2AT

Courses in Forestry

Bangor
University College of North Wales, Bangor, Gwynedd LL57 2DG
Edinburgh
The University, Division of Biological Sciences, West Mains Road, Edinburgh EH9 3JG

Postgraduate Courses
The University of Oxford, Department of Plant Sciences, South Parks Road, Oxford OX1 3RB

Countryside Conservation and Management

First Degree Courses
BSc in Land Management with specialisation in Rural Studies: University of Reading, Faculty of Urban and Regional Studies, Whiteknights, Reading RG6 2AH

BSc in Rural Land Management: University of Reading, Faculty of Urban and Regional Studies, as above. Taught at Royal Agricultural College, Cirencester, Gloucestershire GL7 6JS

BSc (Hons) in Agriculture and Countryside Management: Seale-Hayne Faculty, Polytechnic South West, Faculty of Agriculture, Food and Land Use, Newton Abbot, Devon TQ12 6NQ

BSc (Hons) in Agriculture and Land Management: Royal Agricultural College, as above

BSc (Hons) in Countryside Management: University of Newcastle upon Tyne, Faculty of Agriculture, Newcastle upon Tyne NE1 7RU

BSc (Hons) in Rural Land Management: Royal Agricultural College, as above

BSc (Hons) in Rural Resource Development, with option in Wildlife and Conservation: Writtle College, Chelmsford, Essex CM1 3RR

BSc (Hons) in Rural Resource Management: Seale-Hayne Faculty, Polytechnic South West, as above

BSc (Hons) in Rural Resource Management, University of Newcastle upon Tyne, as above

BSc (Hons) in Rural Resource Management, University of Reading, Department of Agriculture, Earley Gate, PO Box 236, Reading RG6 2AT

BSc/BSc (Hons) in Countryside Management: Wye College, University of London, Wye, Ashford, Kent TN25 5AH

BSc/BSc (Hons) in Rural Enterprise and Land Management: Harper Adams Agricultural College, Newport, Shropshire TF10 8NB

Postgraduate Courses
PGD in Land Resource Management (9 months): Silsoe College, Cranfield Institute of Technology, Silsoe Campus, Bedford MK45 4DT

PGD in Rural Estate Management: Royal Agricultural College, as above

MPhil/AD in Land Management (3 years): University of Reading, Faculty of Urban and Regional Studies, as above

MSc in Conservation of Soil Fertility: Wye College, as above

MSc in Land Resource Management: Silsoe College, as above

MSc in Landscape Ecology, Design and Management: Wye College, as above

MSc in Rural Resources and Environment Policy: Wye College, as above

MSc in Soil Conservation: Silsoe College, as above

Leisure Provision and Management

First Degree Courses

BSc in Rural Resource Management: University College of North Wales, School of Agricultural and Forest Sciences, Memorial Buildings, Bangor, Gwynedd LL57 2UW

BSc (Hons) in Agriculture and Land Management: Royal Agricultural College, Cirencester, Gloucestershire GL7 6JS

BSc (Hons) in Rural Land Management: Royal Agricultural College, as above

BSc (Hons) in Rural Resource Development: Writtle College, Chelmsford, Essex CM1 3RR

BSc (Hons) in Rural Resource Management: Seale-Hayne Faculty, Polytechnic South West, Faculty of Agriculture, Food and Land Use, Newton Abbott, Devon TQ12 6NQ

BSc/BSc (Hons) in Rural Enterprise and Land Management: Harper Adams Agricultural College, Newport, Shropshire TF10 8NB

BSc in Countryside and Environmental Management: University of Aberdeen, Department of Agriculture, 581 King Street, Aberdeen AB9 1UD

Postgraduate Courses

MSc in Land Resource Management: Silsoe College, as above

MSc in Rural Resource Management: University College of North Wales, as above

There are also a number of specialist short courses and courses available to people already employed in conservation. A list of training opportunities can be obtained by writing to the Countryside Commission (address in Chapter 8).

ILAM Certificate (HND level) and Diploma: Institute of Leisure and Amenity Management, Lower Basildon, Reading RG8 9NE

(Courses are run at colleges throughout the country and lead to membership of the Institute. Courses are part time, 2–3 years.)

It is also possible to take higher degrees in agricultural, horticultural and forestry subjects at most of the universities offering first degrees of this kind.

As courses vary considerably in content, you are advised to write to the college or university concerned for a prospectus before making an application for admission.

Courses in Landscape Architecture

The courses marked * provide exemption from all but the final, professional practice part of the Institute of Landscape Architect's examinations (part 4).

First Degree Courses

BA (Hons) in Landscape Design, diploma in Landscape Architecture:* Manchester Polytechnic, All Saints, Manchester M15 6HA
(3-year full-time)

BA in Landscape Architecture:* Leeds Polytechnic, School of the Environment, Brunswick Building, Leeds LS2 8BU
(3-year full-time)

BA (Hons) in Landscape Architecture:* Heriot-Watt University, Department of Architecture, Lauriston Place, Edinburgh EH3 9DF
(4-year full-time)

BSc (Hons) in Natural Environmental Science with Landscape Studies:* Sheffield University, Department of Landscape Architecture, Sheffield S10 2TN
(3-year full-time followed by 1-year full-time diploma/master's degree course in Landscape Architecture)

BSc in Landscape Management: University of Reading, Department of Agriculture and Horticulture, Earley Gate, Reading RG6 2AT
(4-year sandwich)

BA in Landscape Architecture:* Department of Countryside and Landscape, Gloucestershire College of Art and Technology, Francis Close Hall, Swindon Road, Cheltenham, Gloucestershire GL50 4AZ
(4-year full-time)

BA (Hons) and BA in Landscape Architecture:* School of Architecture and Landscape, Thames Polytechnic, Oakfield Lane, Dartford, Kent DA1 2SZ
(3-year full-time)

Postgraduate Courses

MPhil: University of Edinburgh, Department of Architecture, 20 Chambers Street, Edinburgh EH1 1JZ
(2-year full-time)

MPhil (Landscape Design):* University of Newcastle upon Tyne, Department of Town and Country Planning, Newcastle upon Tyne NE1 7RU
(2-year full-time)

Master of Landscape Design; Bachelor of Landscape Design; MA in
Landscape Management: Manchester University, Department of Town
and Country Planning, Manchester M13 9PL
(2-year full-time)

MA in Landscape Design: Sheffield University, Department of Landscape
Architecture, Sheffield S10 2TN
(2-year full-time)

Graduate Diploma in Landscape Architecture: Thames Polytechnic,
School of Architecture and Landscape, Oakfield Lane, Dartford, Kent
DA1 2SZ
(3–5 year part-time)

Graduate Diploma in Landscape Architecture: City of Birmingham Polytechnic, School of Planning and Landscape, Perry Barr, Birmingham
B42 2SU
(3-year part-time)

Courses at Agricultural Colleges

Part-time Courses

Day-release courses are organised for young people aged 16-plus
either through their employer or through Youth Training. These
are based at the agricultural colleges and are slanted towards
practical skills; successful students obtain craft status at the end
of their course. No educational qualifications are required for
taking the courses, but candidates must satisfy the organising
authority that they will benefit from the training. If you are
employed, you will need the co-operation of your employer, who
will usually make the application for you to embark on training.
Most schemes are run under the auspices of local Agricultural
Training Boards, TECs, the Forestry Training Council or the Local
Government Training Board. Most young people taking this form
of training, work for the examinations of the City and Guilds of
London Institute (in Scotland, the Scottish Vocational Education
Council).

These courses are too numerous to list, but details of them are
available locally either from the Regional Training Officer of the
organisation concerned, or from the agricultural colleges. A list of
courses available in Scotland can be obtained from the Scottish
Education Department.

The ATB also runs short in-service courses in a variety of subjects, and courses are available at the Royal Society of Agriculture's
training centre at Kenilworth.

Full-time courses at agricultural colleges are now controlled by the Business and Technician Education Council (BTEC) which validates the qualifications gained by successful students. In Scotland, this is carried out by the Scottish Vocational Education Council (SCOTVEC).

Certificate Courses
One-year full-time certificate courses are run in agriculture, horticulture and forestry for people who have at least one year's practical experience or have successfully completed the first part of a day-release course. They are practically based, but it is helpful if candidates have four GCSE (or equivalent) passes in English, maths and sciences or City and Guilds Part I in agriculture or horticulture.

Successful students are awarded the BTEC National Certificate (NC) and may, if they wish, proceed to more specialised courses.

BTEC National Diploma (ND) Courses
National Diploma (ND) courses are organised on a two-year full-time or a three-year sandwich basis. The sandwich courses last for three years and the middle year is spent working in a setting appropriate to the area of study. Candidates are required to have a BTEC first diploma in a relevant subject *or* at least four GCSE passes, of which one must be in English and two in science subjects *or* NEB Certificate at Credit or Distinction level or equivalent qualification. These courses involve both practical and theoretical work.

BTEC Higher National Diploma (HND) Courses
Higher National Diploma (HND) courses are science-based and are designed for students who wish to work in posts demanding managerial and technological skills. Entrance requirements are *either* one A level in a science subject with appropriate supporting subjects at GCSE (or equivalent) *or* an appropriate BTEC National award. Study is for two years full-time or three years part-time or sandwich study.

List of Agricultural Colleges Offering Full-Time Courses
Further details can be obtained from the prospectuses of individual colleges. All offer general courses in agriculture and horticulture but some offer courses in subjects not commonly available elsewhere and *these only* are indicated in the list.

ENGLAND

Bedfordshire

Shuttleworth Agricultural College, Old Warden Park, Biggleswade SG18 9DX

(NC in farm management)

Silsoe College, Cranfield Institute of Technology, Silsoe Campus, Bedford MK45 4DT

Berkshire

Berkshire College of Agriculture, Hall Place, Burchett's Green, Maidenhead SL6 6QR

(agricultural mechanics)

Cambridgeshire

Cambridgeshire College of Agriculture and Horticulture, Landbeach Road, Milton, Cambridgeshire CB4 6DB

Cambridgeshire College of Agriculture and Horticulture, Newcommon Bridge, Wisbech PE13 2SJ

(1-year full-time course in floristry)

Cheshire

Cheshire College of Agriculture, Reaseheath, Nantwich CW5 6DF

(agricultural engineering)

Cornwall

Duchy College of Agriculture and Horticulture, East Cornwall Centre, Stoke Climsdale, Cellington, Cornwall PL17 8PB

Cumbria

Cumbria College of Agriculture and Forestry, Newton Rigg, Penrith CA11 0AH

(ND and other courses in forestry)

Derbyshire

Broomfield College, Morley, Derby DE7 6DN

Devon

Seale-Hayne Faculty, Polytechnic South West, Newton Abbot TQ12 6NQ

Bicton College of Agriculture, East Budleigh, Budleigh Salterton EX9 7BY

Dorset

Dorset College of Agriculture and Horticulture, Kingston Maurward, Dorchester DT2 8PY

Durham

Houghall College, Durham College of Agriculture and Horticulture, Houghall, Durham DH1 3SG

(ND in land use and recreation)

East Sussex

Plumpton Agricultural College, Plumpton, Lewes BN7 3AE

(C & G agricultural mechanics)

Essex
Writtle College, Writtle, Chelmsford CM1 3RR
Gloucestershire
Royal Agricultural College, Cirencester GL7 6JS
(This is an independent establishment at which courses are not subject
to the usual approval arrangements)
Gloucestershire College of Agriculture and Horticulture, Hartpury House,
Nr Gloucester GL19 3BD
Hampshire
Sparsholt College, Sparsholt, Winchester SO21 2NF
(2-year full-time diploma in fishery studies; 1-year full-time course in
gamekeeping/mechanics)
Hereford and Worcester
Evesham College of Further Education, Cheltenham Road, Evesham
WR11 6LP
(C & G agricultural mechanics/machinery mechanics, ND horticultural
engineering)
Pershore College of Horticulture, Avonbank, Pershore WR10 3JP
(ND in landscape technology)
Holme Lacy College, Holme Lacy, Hereford HR2 6LL
(forestry)
Worcestershire College of Agriculture, Hindlip, Worcester WR3 8SS
Hertfordshire
Oaklands College, St Albans AL4 0JA
Humberside
Bishop Burton College of Agriculture, York Road, Bishop Burton,
Beverley HU17 8QG
(farm management; ND agricultural or horticultural business studies;
machinery and mechanisation; NC in floristry)
Kent
Hadlow College of Agriculture and Horticulture, Hadlow, Tonbridge
TN11 0AL
Wye College, University of London, Wye, Ashford, Kent TN25 5AH
Lancashire
College of Agriculture and Horticulture, Myerscough Hall, Bilsborrow,
Preston PR3 0RY
(NC groundsmanship and greenkeeping; amenity horticulture)
Leicestershire
Brooksby Agricultural College, Brooksby, Melton Mowbray LE14 2LJ
(coarse fish production; country and environmental skills)
Lincolnshire
Lincolnshire College of Agriculture and Horticulture, Caythorpe Court,
Grantham NG32 3EP
(agricultural engineering; arable mechanisation; forestry)

London

Capel Manor Horticultural and Environmental Centre, Bullsmoor Lane, Enfield, Middlesex EN1 4RQ

Norwood Hall Institute of Horticultural Education, Norwood Green, Southall, Middlesex UB2 4LA

Norfolk

Norfolk College of Agriculture and Horticulture, Easton, Norwich NR9 5DX

Northamptonshire

Moulton College of Agriculture and Horticulture, Moulton, Northampton NN3 1RR

Northumberland

Kirkley Hall College, Ponteland, Newcastle upon Tyne NE20 0AQ
  (agricultural mechanics; land use and reclamation)

North Yorkshire

Askham Bryan College, Askham Bryan, York YO2 3PR
  (ND in amenity horticulture with an option in arboriculture. HND in landscape and horticultural technology)

Nottinghamshire

Brackenhurst College, Southwell NG25 0QF
  (National Certificate with an arable farming bias; C & G agricultural engineering)

Oxfordshire

Rycotewood College, Priest End, Thame OX9 2BR
  (ND agricultural engineering)

Oxfordshire Agricultural Education Centre, Warren Farm, Horton-cum-Studley OX9 1BY

West Oxfordshire College, Holloway Road, Witney OX8 7EE

Shropshire

Harper Adams Agricultural College, Newport TF10 8NB

Walford College of Agriculture, Walford, Baschurch, Shrewsbury SY4 2HL
  (farm management course)

Somerset

Cannington College, Cannington, Nr Bridgwater TA5 2LS
  (amenity horticulture; agricultural mechanics)

Staffordshire

Staffordshire College of Agriculture, Rodbaston, Penkridge, Stafford ST19 5PH

Suffolk

Otley College of Agriculture and Horticulture, Otley, Ipswich IP6 9EY

Surrey

Merrist Wood Agricultural College, Worplesdon, Nr Guildford GU3 3PE
(NC and ND courses in arboriculture. ND course in countryside recreation.
Short courses in tree surgery; machinery mechanics)

Warwickshire

Warwickshire College of Agriculture, Moreton Hall, Moreton Morrell,
Warwick CV35 9BL
(C & G agricultural mechanics)

West Sussex

West Sussex College of Agriculture and Horticulture, Brinsbury, North
Heath, Pulborough RH20 1DL
(C & G agricultural mechanics; floristry)

Wiltshire

Lackham College, Lacock, Chippenham SN15 2NY
(agricultural machinery; agricultural engineering technician)

WALES

Clwyd

Llysfasi College of Agriculture, Ruthin, Clwyd LL15 2LB

The Welsh College of Horticulture, Northop, Nr Mold, Clwyd CH7 6AA
(ND and other courses in floristry and flower production; NC in
amenity horticulture; 1-year full-time course in landscape construction;
machinery and mechanisation)

Dyfed

Carmarthen College of Technology and Art, Agriculture Department,
Golden Grove Campus, Golden Grove, Carmarthen SA32 8LR
(farm tourism option with NC in agriculture; C & G agricultural
mechanics; ND in business studies in agricultural industry; agricultural
engineering)

Welsh Agricultural College, Llanbadarn Fawr, Aberystwyth SY23 3AL

Gwynedd

Glynllifon College, Clynnog Road, Caernarvon LL54 5DU

Gwent

The Usk College of Agriculture, Usk NP5 1XJ

Mid-Glamorgan

Mid-Glamorgan College of Agriculture and Horticulture, Pencoed,
Bridgend CF35 5LG
(amenity horticulture)

Powys

Montgomery College of Further Education, Newtown SY16 1BE

SCOTLAND

Borders

Borders College of Further Education, Thorniedean, Melrose Road, Galashiels TD1 2AF

Dumfries and Galloway

The Barony College, Parkgate, Dumfries DG1 3NE
(SCOTVEC National Certificate (SNC) in agricultural engineering, fish farming)

Fife

Elmwood Agricultural and Technical College, Carslogie Road, Cupar, Fife KY15 4HY
(SCOTVEC certificates in greenkeeping; arboriculture; agricultural engineering; amenity supervision)

Grampian

University of Aberdeen, Department of Agriculture, 581 King Street, Aberdeen AB9 1UD

Clinterty Agricultural College, Kinellar, Aberdeenshire AB5 0TN
(agricultural engineering)

Highland

Scottish School of Forestry, Inverness College of Further and Higher Education, 3 Longman Road, Inverness IV1 1SA
(SCOTVEC diploma and certificate in forestry)

Thurso Technical College, Ormlie Road, Thurso, Caithness KW14 7EE
(forest ranger; gamekeeping)

Lothian

University of Edinburgh, School of Agriculture, West Mains Road, Edinburgh EH9 3JG

Oatridge Agricultural College, Ecclesmachan, Broxburn, West Lothian EH52 6NH
(YT course in forestry. SCOTVEC certificates in farm management; gamekeeping and groundsmanship; agricultural engineering; amenity horticulture; YT in forestry and agricultural engineering)

Orkney Islands Area

Kirkwall Further Education Centre, Kirkwall, Orkney
(SCOTVEC certificate in farm management; NC in agricultural engineering)

Strathclyde

The Scottish Agricultural College (Edinburgh, Aberdeen and Ayr) Academic Registry, Freepost, Ayr
(HND agricultural engineering)

Kilmarnock College, Holehouse Road, Kilmarnock KA3 7AT

Motherwell College, Dalzell Drive, Motherwell ML1 2DD

Langside College, Department of Horticulture, Woodburn House, Buchanan Drive, Rutherglen G73 3PF

Stirlingshire

Falkirk College of Technology, Orangemouth Road, Falkirk, Stirlingshire FK2 9AD

Tayside

Angus College of Further Education, Keptie Road, Arbroath, Angus DD11 3EA

Dundee College of Further Education, Kingsway Centre, Old Glamis Road, Dundee DD3 8LE

Perth College of Further Education, Braham Estate, Crieff Road, Perth PH1 2NX

(agricultural engineering)

NORTHERN IRELAND

Antrim

Greenmount Agricultural and Horticultural College, 22 Greenmount Road, Antrim BT41 4PU

County Fermanagh

Enniskillen Agricultural College, Irvinestown Road, Enniskillen BT746DN

County Tyrone

Loughry College of Agriculture and Food Technology, Cookstown BT80 9AA

(Diploma in communication studies)

Other Courses

Turf Culture and Groundsmanship

Institute of Groundsmanship, 19–23 Church Street, The Agora, Wolverton, Milton Keynes MK12 5LG

(Certificate and diploma examinations in turf culture and sportsground management – open to all practising groundsmen)

A list of colleges participating in the certificates is available from the Institute.

The Sports Turf Research Institute, Bingley, West Yorkshire BD16 1AU

(Courses in the theory and practice of turf construction and management)

Horticulture

Royal Botanic Garden, Edinburgh EH3 5LR

(3-year diploma in amenity and ornamental horticulture)

Applicants must be between the ages of 19 and 23 and already possess a horticultural qualification at National Certificate or National Diploma level as well as at least four GCSEs or equivalent. Students take part in the day-to-day work of the garden and receive formal training for one day each week.

Royal Botanic Gardens, Kew, Richmond, Surrey TW9 3AB
(3-year course in general horticulture leading to the Kew Diploma)
Entry requirements are five passes in suitable subjects at GCSE and two
A levels as well as two years' practical experience. Students must be
at least 18 when they begin their course. No fees are charged and a
subsistence allowance is paid for work on the upkeep of the gardens.

The National Trust runs Youth Training courses under the Training
Scheme in basic horticulture for school leavers. Inquiries should be made
to your nearest National Trust office.

National Trust for Scotland, Threave School of Gardening, Castle
Douglas, Dumfries and Galloway, Scotland DG7 1RX
(2-year full-time course leading to the Threave Diploma)
There are no minimum educational requirements but students must have
completed at least one year's full-time horticultural work.

Up-to-date details of courses in horticulture are given in certain issues of
the magazine *Horticulture Week*.

Arboriculture

Certificate and National Diploma in Arboriculture, awarded by the
Royal Forestry Society. Courses in arboriculture are run at Askham
Bryan College, York; Capel Manor Institute of Horticulture and
Field Studies, Bullsmoor Lane, Waltham Cross, Hertfordshire;
Cheshire College of Agriculture, Reaseheath, Nantwich, Cheshire;
and Merrist Wood Agricultural College, Worplesdon, Guildford,
Surrey. The three-year diploma course in horticulture at the Royal
Botanic Gardens, Kew, Richmond, Surrey includes tree work and
is practically orientated. A similar course is run at the Royal
Botanic Garden, Edinburgh.

Working Overseas

A period of time spent working in a developing country can
be a rewarding experience as well as a valuable contribution to
the country concerned. Anyone with a formal qualification in
agriculture, horticulture or forestry and some practical experience
may be suited to the work, but there is also a need for people with
more specialised higher training.

Reading University runs two postgraduate courses in tropical
agricultural development and the Overseas Development Administration offers a wide range of postgraduate studentships listed in
their booklet 'Postgraduate Training Awards Scheme'.

For a list of agencies through which overseas work can be arranged, see Chapter 8.

Applying for a Course

Universities have their own clearing house scheme (see p 91) but applications for full-time courses at agricultural colleges should be made direct to the colleges concerned. Initial inquiries should be made to the secretary of the college well in advance of the proposed start of studies, usually in the autumn preceding the beginning of the next academic year. Addresses of Agricultural Training Board offices are given in Chapter 8.

Most agricultural colleges will help with general careers advice and give information about the most suitable courses for individual people.

Grants

Maintenance grants and student loans are statutory for students accepted for degree and HND courses, provided they have been resident in the UK for three years immediately before they begin their studies. Grants for people taking other full-time courses are discretionary. Many local authorities are willing to provide them, although they may insist that you attend your local college if it offers a suitable course. All grants are on a sliding scale based upon parental income. Inquiries should be made to your local education authority at the time you apply for a course. In Scotland, applications for statutory grants should be made to the Scottish Education Department (see p 108 for address) and for discretionary grants to your regional education authority. For a leaflet on grants and awards, write to Warwickshire County Council Careers Service, 22 Northgate Street, Warwick CV34 4SR.

Chapter 8

Useful Addresses

General

The Universities Central Council on Admissions (UCCA), PO Box 28, Cheltenham, Gloucestershire GL50 3SA

Business and Technician Education Council, Central House, Upper Woburn Place, London WC1H 0HH

City and Guilds of London Institute, 76 Portland Place, London W1N 4AA

Scottish Vocational Education Council, Hanover House, 24 Douglas Street, Glasgow G2 7NQ

The Agricultural Training Board

The local ATB offices will help with inquiries about training and opportunities for practical work experience. Inquiries should be addressed to the Agricultural or Horticultural Advisory Officer.

Anglia ATB, 9 Willow Lane, Norwich, Norfolk NR2 1EY

Central ATB, 17 Town Street, Duffield, Derby DE6 4EH

Devon and Cornwall ATB, Trinity Court, Southernhay East, Exeter, Devon EX1 1PD

Heart of England ATB, York House, Clarendon Avenue, Leamington Spa CV32 5PP

Kent and East Sussex ATB, 21 Stone Street, Cranbrook, Kent TN17 3HE

Lancashire and Cheshire ATB, Council Offices, High Street, Garstang, Preston PR3 1EB

Lincolnshire and Humberside ATB, Abbey House, Castlegate, Grantham, Lincolnshire NG31 6SE

Mid Wessex ATB, 31 Trull Road, Taunton, Somerset TA1 4QG

Midwest ATB, 7 Raven Lane, Ludlow, Shropshire SY8 1BW

North of England ATB, 4th Floor, Cathedral Buildings, Dean Street, Newcastle upon Tyne NE1 1PQ

ATB Scotland, Highland House, St Catherine's Road, Perth PH1 5YA

Southern ATB, 59 London Road, Horsham, West Sussex RH12 1AN

Thames ATB, 11–12 East Lockinge, Wantage, Oxfordshire OX12 8QG
ATB Wales, Llanelwedd, Builth Wells, Powys LD2 3SY
West Anglia ATB, Phoenix House, 67A High Street, Haverhill, Suffolk
    CB9 8AH
Yorkshire ATB, Princes House, 13 Princes Square, Harrogate, North
    Yorkshire HG1 1LW
National Association of Agricultural Contractors, Huts Corner, Tilford
    Road, Hindhead, Surrey GU26 6SF
National Proficiency Tests Council, Tenth Street, National Agricultural
    Centre, Stoneleigh Park, Kenilworth CV8 2LG
National Examinations Board for Agriculture, Horticulture and Allied
    Industries, 46 Britannia Street, London WC1X 9RG
Royal Agricultural Society/Warwickshire County Council Careers Service,
    10 Northgate Street, Warwick CV34 4SR
East Anglian Regional Advisory Council for Further Education, 2 Looms
    Lane, Bury St Edmunds, Suffolk IP33 1HE
General Inquiries – Scotland
The Scottish Education Department, New St Andrews House, Edinburgh
    EH1 3SI
Women's Farm and Garden Association, 175 Gloucester Street,
    Cirencester GL7 2DP

Agriculture

Ministry of Agriculture, Fisheries and Food, Personnel Division, Victory
    House, 30–34 Kingsway, London WC2B 6TU (For information about
    careers in ADAS)
National Dairy Council, Education Department, 5–7 John Princes
    Street, London W1M 0AP (For brochure 'Looking Ahead – Careers
    in the Dairy Industry')
National Farmers' Union, Agriculture House, Knightsbridge, London
    SW1X 7NJ
National Farmers' Union of Scotland, 17 Grosvenor Crescent, Edinburgh
    EH12 5EN
The National Association of Agricultural Contractors, Huts Corner,
    Tilford Road, Hindhead, Surrey GU26 6SF

Horticulture

The Royal Horticultural Society, PO Box 313, 80 Vincent Square, London
    SW1P 2PE (For free booklet 'Come into Horticulture')

Institute of Groundsmanship, 19–23 Church Street, The Agora, Wolverton, Milton Keynes MK12 5LG

The Landscape Institute, 6–7 Barnard Mews, London SW11 1QU

Institute of Leisure and Amenity Management, ILAM House, Lower Basildon, Reading, Berkshire RG8 9NE

Local Government Training Board, 8 The Arndale Centre, Luton, Bedfordshire LU1 2PS

Forestry

Aboricultural Association, Ampfield House, Ampfield, Nr Romsey, Hampshire SO51 9PA

Association of Professional Foresters, Brokerswood House, Brokerswood, Westbury, Wiltshire BA13 4EH

Forestry Commission (Training and Headquarters), 231 Corstorphine Road, Edinburgh EH12 7AT

Forestry Training Council, Room 413, 231 Corstophine Road, Edinburgh EH12 7AT

Institute of Chartered Foresters, 22 Walker Street, Edinburgh EH3 7HR

Royal Forestry Society of England, Wales and Northern Ireland, 102 High Street, Tring, Hertfordshire HP23 4AH

Royal Scottish Forestry Society, 10 Atholl Crescent, Edinburgh EH3 8HA

Timber Growers United Kingdom, Admel House, 24 High Street, Wimbledon, London SW19 5DX

Conservation

British Trust for Conservation Volunteers (BTCV), 36 St Mary's Street, Wallingford OX10 0EH

(The Trust runs and finances a voluntary field force and will advise anyone wanting to undertake voluntary work.)

The Countryside Commission, John Dower House, Crescent Place, Cheltenham, Gloucestershire GL50 3RA

The Countryside Commission (Publications) for its *Countryside* Education and Training Directory; 19–23 Albert Road, Manchester M19 2EQ

The Countryside Commission for Scotland, Battleby, Redgorton, Perth PH1 3EW

Countryside Council for Wales, Plas Penrhos, Ffordd Penrhos, Bangor, Gwynedd LLF7 2LQ

English Nature, Nature Conservancy Council for England, Northminster House, Peterborough PE1 1UA

National Rivers Authority, 30–34 Albert Embankment, London SE1 7TL

The National Trust, 36 Queen Anne's Gate, London SW1H 9AS

The National Trust for Scotland, 5 Charlotte Square, Edinburgh EH2 4DU

Nature Conservancy Council for Scotland, 12 Hope Terrace, Edinburgh EH9 2AS

The Royal Society for Nature Conservation, The Green, Witham Park, Waterside South, Lincoln LN5 7JR

(The Society will supply a list of Wildlife Trusts.)

Royal Society for the Protection of Birds

Headquarters: The Lodge, Sandy, Bedfordshire SG19 2DL

Scottish Office: 17 Regent Terrace, Edinburgh EH7 5BN

Welsh Office: Bryn Aderyn, The Bank, Newtown, Powys SY16 2AB

A full list of the many charitable and voluntary associations active in the field of nature conservation is available from the Nature Conservancy Council (Information Sheet No 2).

Some postgraduate courses may receive support from the Natural Environment Research Council.

Inquiries to: University Support Section, Natural Environment Research Council, Polaris House, North Star Avenue, Swindon SN2 1EV

Land agents are members of the Royal Institution of Chartered Surveyors.

Inquiries to: The Careers Department, The Royal Institution of Chartered Surveyors, 12 Great George Street, Parliament Square, London SW1P 3AE.

Additional Addresses

Association of Countryside Rangers, ILAM House, Lower Basildon, Reading, Berkshire RG8 9NE

British Council, 10 Spring Gardens, London SW1A 2BN (for training overseas)

Commonwealth Development Corporation, 33 Hill Street, London W1A 2AR

Commonwealth Secretariat, Education Programme, Marlborough House, Pall Mall, London SW1Y 5HX

The Institute of Agricultural Engineers, West End Road, Silsoe, Bedford MK45 4DU

The International Exchange of Young Agriculturalists, The Secretary, National Federation of Young Farmers Clubs, National Agriculture Centre, Stoneleigh, Kenilworth, Warwickshire CV8 2LZ (Operates an exchange scheme for people aged 18–26 with two years' practical experience. Successful candidates are placed in Europe, North America, Australia and New Zealand for three to twelve months.)

Overseas Development Administration, International Recruitment Unit, Abercrombie House, Eaglesham Road, East Kilbride, Glasgow G75 8EA

The Scottish Education Department (Awards Branch), Gyleview House, 3 Redheughs Rigg, South Gyle, Edinburgh EH12 9HH